REAL ESTATE CAREER STARTER

REAL ESTATE
career starter

2nd edition

Mary Masi

with Lauren B. Starkey

LEARNINGEXPRESS

New York

Printed in the United States of America
9 8 7 6 5 4 3 2
Second Edition

ISBN 1-57685-370-5

Regarding the Information in this Book

Every effort has been made to ensure the accuracy of directory information up until press time. However, phone numbers and/or addresses are subject to change. Please contact the respective organization for the most recent information.

For Further Information

For more information or to place an order, contact LearningExpress at:

55 Broadway
8th Floor
New York, NY 10006

Or visit us at:

www.learnatest.com

Contents

Contents

Introduction

Why Enter the Real Estate Field?

ARE YOU looking for the opportunity to earn a good living, meet interesting people, and have flexible work hours? Would you enjoy learning new things, working with the latest communications technology, and having no two days alike? If so, a career in real estate may be a great fit for you. Real estate careers can be both personally and financially rewarding, as you help others find the home of their dreams, and get paid for doing so.

There are always opportunities in real estate. Most openings occur because of replacement needs; some in the field move on to other occupations, and others leave the work force. Indeed, the Bureau of Labor Statistics notes that those working in real estate are older on average than other occupations. Other opportunities become available when brokers open new offices that need to be staffed. In real estate, you'll be working with one of life's basic necessities, shelter, so the need for your services will never go away!

This book will help you every step of the way, from deciding whether to pursue a position in real estate, to getting educated and licensed, to landing your first job and succeeding in it. Along the way, you'll get inside information from those already working in the field.

In Chapter 1, you'll get an overview of the real estate field. You'll learn about the different types of sales agents and brokers, and what spells success for each type of position. Included is an update on educational trends, and those areas of the country experiencing the fastest growth. There is also an opportunity for you to take a quiz in order to find out if a career in real estate is right for you.

Chapter 2 explains in detail the educational opportunities available to those planning a career as a real estate professional. You'll see several real estate program descriptions from a number of schools, and learn how to evaluate training programs (a listing of training programs in each state is included in Appendix C). You'll also read about online educational opportunities, continuing education, and professional designations.

In Chapter 3, we cover the important topic of licensing. Every state in the country requires its agents and brokers to be licensed before they can participate in any real estate business. From our comprehensive listing of state licensing requirements, you'll not only be able to learn what your state expects of you, but you'll be able to compare those requirements with those from other states. Included is contact information, including street addresses, phone numbers, and websites, for each agency.

Chapter 4 will tell you how to get employed once you've completed your real estate education and received your license. Your job search is outlined in detail, from finding out who's hiring, to writing your resume and cover letters. The interview process, and use of the Internet for job searching are also discussed.

The last chapter shows how you can succeed once you've landed a job. You'll get plenty of advice from those already in the field, on topics such as using the latest technology and fitting in with the people in your office. Also covered are how best to interact with superiors and the public, and how to increase your level of success. Chapter 5 ends with information on advancement opportunities and career options.

Once you've read through this book, you'll have the knowledge you need to get started on your path toward a career in real estate. Success in this exciting field can be yours. Good luck!

REAL ESTATE CAREER STARTER

CHAPTER one

CHOOSING A CAREER IN REAL ESTATE

IN THIS chapter, you'll get an overview of the real estate field. You'll learn what makes a successful sales agent, the latest educational trends, and where the most jobs are. We've also included job descriptions in real estate sales and brokerage, and the minimum requirements needed to launch a lucrative career in each of them. Plus, each area of specialization is clearly explained: residential, commercial, industrial, farms, and farmland. Then, find out if a career in real estate is right for you by taking the quiz at the end of this chapter.

THE OPPORTUNITIES available in the real estate field today are many and varied. Few other careers offer the excitement, challenges, and income potential that this promising field does. Once you begin a career in real estate, you'll be a part of one of the largest industries in America today. According to the Bureau of Labor Statistics, there were over 347,000 jobs in real estate in 1998, and they predict that through the next decade, jobs in real estate sales will be especially plentiful. This is due to the large number of people who leave the real estate field every year, many of whom are not willing to work full-time. With the advances in technology, and increasing legal issues facing agents and brokers, it usually takes full-time hours to keep up and become successful.

Many jobs in the real estate field can be yours with a minimum of training, so you can get started on your path to success right away. That's one of the advantages of working in real estate, and that reason—along with the high income potential—draws many people, both recent graduates who want to begin a new career fresh out of school, and career-changers. On the other hand, many people today are pursuing college degrees in real estate and are entering the field with a solid educational background. The possibilities are endless in this diverse and gratifying field.

Numerous demands are placed on real estate professionals, and they often must wear many hats in the course of their workdays. These demands might include working odd hours, or answering a frantic phone call late at night from a seller, agonizing over a buyer's offer. Keeping up with technology as it affects the field is done through continuing education, often on agents' "down time," in a home office. Regulations and other ever-changing and more complex legal issues relating to real estate also keep those in the field constantly learning. As Lydia Wisloski, an agent in Essex, Vermont, says:

> It's easy to keep your interest level and motivation up. There are so many types of land and housing, zoning laws, personalities of small towns, property rights, and environmental laws and regulations to learn about and keep up with. It is a fascinating field, and every situation, every deal, is different.

WHY ENTER THE REAL ESTATE FIELD?

There are a number of reasons why so many people are attracted to the field of real estate. An obvious benefit of real estate sales is the chance to make high commissions and earn a good living. Many sales agents also say they enjoy the chance to meet new people and the variety of their workdays. Others value the excitement of the "deal," always trying to get first crack at new listings of homes for sale, and then negotiating the best deal for their client. A large number of sales agents and brokers own real estate property for investment purposes, and they know enough about the business to make informed decisions on what property to buy and where. These are just a few of the many reasons agents and brokers cite when asked what they love about their work.

Flexible Work Schedule for Sales Agents

One of the reasons many people decide to get into real estate sales is because they do not want to sit behind a desk in an office job and work 9-to-5, five days a week. The variety of the real estate professional's work schedule appeals to people who want flexibility and variety in their work tasks. However, don't mistake flexibility with shorter hours. While agents may schedule their first meeting with a client at 10:00 a.m. in order to attend a child's school conference, they may also have to show a home at 8:00 that evening.

In 1998, according to the Bureau of Labor Statistics, one out of four agents and brokers worked at least 50 hours a week. This statistic is verified by the many professionals interviewed for this book. While real estate was once considered a great career option for part-timers, there are a number of factors causing the field to trend away from part-time employees. Technology allows listings to be available almost immediately to every agent in the country. As soon as it hits the computer, everyone—including prospective homebuyers—has access. You need to be alert and aware to catch great properties for your clients as they come up. As Don and Bert Marcy, a husband-and-wife agent team for over 20 years, note:

> "You need to make a commitment, and be serious about taking responsibility for someone else's hopes and dreams. This is no place for a dabbler. If you're not willing to invest the time to do the job right, don't do it at all. There is too much at stake to do otherwise." Don concurs, "Bert is absolutely right. You need to make a commitment. That doesn't mean you have to make it your 40-hour-a-week job; it just means you shouldn't try to do another job and sell real estate too."

Autonomy for Brokers

Brokers who own their own real estate company enjoy a great level of autonomy. Their status as owners often brings them a high level of job satisfaction. While the pressures are high when you are the boss, so are the benefits of not having to answer to anyone else. For those brokers who are experienced and successful, their level of autonomy gives them great pleasure. (Of course, if you are floundering and profits are falling, you might prefer to pin it all on someone else instead of yourself.) A broker in St. Paul, Minnesota sums it up this way:

> I always wanted to work for myself, and I really hated having to punch a clock at my old job in my previous career as a car service manager. It was my incessant drive for autonomy that helped me to make it through the lean years when I was struggling to get listings and sell homes when I first came into real estate. Now, after 11 years as a salesman and three as a broker, I feel that I have finally achieved my dream. I am my own boss, and I love it. I answer to no one.

Hard Work Is Rewarded for Sales Agents

In the real estate business, the people who are rewarded are the ones who bring in the most and biggest commissions. Therefore, your rewards are in direct relation to your hard work. As you gain experience, contacts, and referrals, you'll find that you have more bargaining power with your broker and may be able to negotiate a more favorable commission split. Lydia Wislowski, an agent in Vermont, says:

> Our broker uses commission splits as an incentive. For example, for all sales up to 1 million dollars, you might receive a 50-50 split. From 1 million to 2.5 million, your part of the commission might increase to 60 percent. When your total sales exceed 5 million, your share is even higher.

Your "reward" for hard work won't just be more money in your pocket, however. Depending on the office in which you work, you might receive sales awards, and get favorable treatment such as a better desk or office space and less "floor time." While rewards very greatly from office to office, be assured that if you are closing a high number of transactions, your broker will treat you favorably.

Ease of Entrance from Another Career for Sales Agents/Brokers

Historically, real estate was a career that people came to later in life. Many sales agents made a transition into real estate from another career, such as office manager, sales representative, teacher, or homemaker (read through the "Inside Track" features at the end of each chapter for a sampling). Donna Dawson, an agent in California, is making the transition from teaching to real estate sales:

> I have been selling real estate part-time while teaching in high school. However, I am eager to be able to concentrate on only one job soon. I am retiring from teaching next year to sell real estate full-time, making a career change while I still have the energy and enthusiasm to pursue it.

Recently, more and more people are majoring in real estate in college and are making real estate their first career. However, there are still many career-changers who enter the real estate field from a variety of other backgrounds. One of the reasons so many career-changers choose real estate is the ease of entrance requirements.

Most states require applicants to take a limited number of hours of real estate courses and pass a written exam before they can get their license to practice real estate sales (find your state's requirements in Chapter 3). These requirements can often be met within a few months if you study on a regular basis and dutifully apply yourself to learning the material. Also, if you are entering real estate from a career in which you had considerable public contact, you may already have a wealth of possible contacts for getting listings and for selling properties. Don't underestimate the value of your current networking contacts for a new career in real estate.

Chance to Become Self-Employed

Many real estate professionals are self-employed, so they enjoy more freedom than employees who have a boss to whom they must answer. Most sales agents work as independent contractors for their sponsoring broker. For those sales agents who apply themselves and pass the required courses and exam for becoming a broker, the possibilities just keep expanding. In many states, you can work for yourself as a broker in a one-person operation. This would mean keeping 100% of your commissions! You can even branch out after a few years and open your own office or buy into a real estate franchise opportunity and hire other sales agents to work for you, so you can get a percentage of the commissions they earn as well.

In addition to sales agents and brokers, a significant number of real estate appraisers and property managers also work for themselves. In fact, almost half of all property managers were self-employed in 1998, according to the Bureau of Labor Statistics. Therefore, many entrepreneurial types are interested in becoming real estate professionals.

IN THE NEWS

Will building denser housing curb suburban sprawl? A survey by the National Association of Realtors showed that 73% of those surveyed said they wouldn't think about buying a home on a smaller lot, closer to neighbors' homes. However, many conceded that they would accept greater densities if there were plans to include more attractive homes, parks, trees, and sidewalks.

DO YOU HAVE WHAT IT TAKES?

What does it take to become a success in the real estate field today? We asked sales agents, brokers, appraisers, and property managers for their opinions. Their summarized answers follow.

Motivation

A certain amount of motivation is needed for performing almost any job. However, in real estate, it's of the utmost importance. Many real estate positions are in essence self-employed ones, meaning you won't have an employer urging you on to succeed. The drive to work hard needs to come from within you. If you need to have someone constantly reminding you to do something or if you feel that you tend toward procrastination, you may need to invest some time and money in motivation seminars if you want to succeed, especially in real estate sales.

Persistence

Being persistent can help you succeed in reaching any goal. In real estate, it's an especially important quality to have when times get tough. You'll encounter many deals in which conflicts arise or roadblocks pop up from out of nowhere. Perhaps it's the overbearing father-in-law who insists a particular house is not right for the young couple who have already signed the contract on the house and adore it. Or maybe a broker/owner is having trouble making ends meet during the first year of the new business. It is during these times that persistence becomes especially important.

For a self-employed appraiser who is building up a client list, persistence can mean the difference between a thriving business in a couple of years, or a dead end. It takes time and effort to achieve success in this challenging field; many real estate professionals will tell you that their success took off only after they'd been in the field for a few years. It was during the early years of laying the groundwork—putting in the time to get to know a neighborhood, making contacts, building a list of referrals, and advertising consistently—that persistence was key.

Good Communication Skills

All real estate professionals need strong communication skills because they're in a people-oriented business. Appraisers need to be able to communicate well, both verbally and in writing, because they spend hours conducting research, interviewing people, and writing reports. Those reports need to be clear and understandable to their target audience. Property managers also need to possess good communication skills because they are the conduits of information between tenants and owners. They must know how to interact with and please both sides. A property manager from Chicago, Illinois describes it this way:

> It's definitely a challenge. You constantly have to figure out ways to negotiate and mediate so each party feels that you are looking out for them. Of course, your main responsibility is to the owners since they are paying you to manage their property. But it is an extension of that very responsibility that requires you to try and satisfy the tenants as well. If the tenants are happy, they pay their rent on time and the building stays occupied. If you get the tenants angry or can't calm them down or help them when they need you, they may leave and then you'll be stuck trying to explain that to the owners. So it's all a delicate balancing act that requires tact, good listening skills, and the ability to be objective and unemotional in the face of confrontation.

Mathematical Ability

Working with numbers is an important aspect of any real estate professional's job duties. For instance, the real estate licensing exam for sales agents and brokers normally devotes at least 25% of the total number of questions to real estate math computations. As a sales agent, you will need to help clients to figure out how much they can afford to spend on a home by looking at their income, assets, and debts. You may even help them apply for a mortgage. It's important to be sure that you are not showing $125,000 houses to a family that can't afford anything above $90,000. This would be a waste not only of your time, but a waste of the sellers' and potential buyers' time as well.

However, don't let a lack of math skills scare you off from a career in real estate. You can probably master most, if not all, of the math skills you need to pass the real estate licensing exam if you study and practice the skills every day. Several good books are available to help you learn and improve the math skills needed to pass the state licensing exam—see Appendix A for a list of relevant titles.

Attention to Detail

There are many laws and regulations governing the sale of property; most of them carry stiff penalties for those who ignore them. You need to understand and keep fair housing and zoning laws in mind, as well as environmental laws and regulations. If you're showing a house to a couple with three children, and its septic system is designed only for four people, you could have a serious problem if you don't alert them to this fact. Disclosure laws mandate that you, and the seller of a property, tell a buyer about any problem or potential problem with that property, so you need to be sure you have done your homework thoroughly (see Just the Facts about radon on the following page for an example).

In addition to legal issues, there is an enormous stack of paperwork necessary for every transaction in which you are involved. In order for a closing to take place, you will need to attend to many details carefully. This attention to detail is also critical for appraisers. A real estate appraiser from Atlanta, Georgia, describes the importance of details in this way:

> If I were to lose track of one little piece of information during the appraisal process, it could mean an alteration of the final estimate of value on the property. It is amazing how important each little detail is in this profession. It could be one clause in a zoning ordinance, or one mistake in a measurement taken, or missing something on a public record that could skew the end result. That's why I am painstakingly careful, and retrace all my steps for each project to make sure every detail is correct and accounted for. You must be able to focus on the details and follow-up on each one to be sure you get the best estimate possible for each property you appraise.

JUST THE FACTS

For years, it was possible for sellers to hide negative information about their property from buyers. In some instances, this information could prove deadly, which is one of the reasons disclosure laws have been enacted around the country, making it a crime for sellers and their agents to willfully keep knowledge of any problem, or potential problem, from the seller. One of the deadliest of these problems has been radon. Radon is an invisible, odorless, radioactive gas found in nature that exists in varying amounts in soil. It can enter homes through cracks or holes in concrete floors or walls, sump pits, and drinking water from private wells. Once trapped inside an enclosed space, radon can accumulate. Long-term exposure to radon is the second leading cause of lung cancer in the United States and is estimated to cause thousands of deaths per year, according to the EPA (Environmental Protection Agency). Now, radon testing is a routine part of a home-inspection report, and most lending institutions will not close on a property without first getting the results of such testing.

Honesty

Many real estate professionals list honesty as the number one personal attribute needed in the real estate field. Due to the large amounts of money involved in each real estate transaction (indeed, many deals consist of a person's lifetime savings), honesty is of the utmost importance. However, many realtors are quick to say that in this regard, their profession is no different from any other. Although real estate did have a reputation for dishonesty, those in the field say it was mostly undeserved. Roberta Dinerstein notes:

> Our national organization, the National Association of REALTORS® (NAR), has helped to turn around the negative public perceptions of our field. For many years, the real estate profession had some bad PR, some of it deserved, and some not. I don't think we're any different from other professions; I don't believe the slogan "buyer beware" should be used in real estate any more than it should be used when hiring an attorney, architect, or doctor. I've found that those who stay in our business support honest dealing with the public. They work under the NAR Code of Ethics.

Ability to Handle Rejection and Disappointment

After spending many hours driving buyers around to look at home after home, a sales agent may find out that the buyers decided to purchase a home that was for sale by an owner. Or perhaps the buyer's cousin just obtained his real estate license, so they bought it through him instead. Agents must be able to handle this disappointment in a constructive way and realize that it's all a part of the job. Some degree of uncertainty exists when working in this field and things won't always work out the way you'd like them to. Even if you invest considerable time and effort into making a sale, obstacles arise that may be out of your control. Therefore, you need to be able to move on and not let the disappointments get you down. Resiliency is an important characteristic of successful real estate sales agents.

Management Skills

Brokers and office managers who own or run a real estate office must have good management skills. It is not enough just to know how to sell real estate.

One of the most common ways to obtain management training and improve these skills is to take courses in business management and finance from your local community college or university. Some of the franchise real estate companies offer in-house management training to their office managers and brokers. The NAR also offers education in management. Take advantage of any training opportunities that arise if you think you might want to get into management—it could be one of the keys to your success.

EDUCATIONAL TRENDS

Real estate professionals are increasingly obtaining higher levels of education than they have in the past. Indeed, many now have some college education, whether it is only a few courses, an associate degree, a bachelor's degree, or even in some cases, a master's or doctorate degree in real estate or a related area. While a college degree is not required to become a real estate sales agent or broker, you could benefit from taking college-level courses. Studies in the following subject areas are especially useful to those planning to enter the real estate field:

- ▶ Real estate
- ▶ Finance
- ▶ Economics
- ▶ Marketing
- ▶ Business administration
- ▶ Psychology
- ▶ Sociology
- ▶ Architecture
- ▶ Engineering

In addition to college courses, many private schools offer real estate training specifically tailored to help you pass the licensing exam in your state. See Chapter 2 for more detailed information about the types of training programs and educational courses and degrees that are available, and how you can choose the one that's best for you.

JUST THE FACTS

Most states require salesperson and broker applicants to have a minimum of a high school diploma or General Equivalency Diploma (GED). They then issue licenses only to those who successfully complete a specified number of hours of pre-licensing education, and renew licenses only to those who take approved continuing education courses. The exceptions include Missouri, which does not require a high school education of its applicants, and New Jersey, which does not have a continuing education requirement for license renewal.

FAST-GROWING GEOGRAPHIC LOCATIONS

If you don't mind relocating in your quest for a successful career in real estate, there are areas of the country that are growing and are in need of real estate professionals. As you might guess, California remains first in the nation for the number and cost of real estate deals. Other states that have a growing need include Florida, Nevada, and Texas.

In addition to the southern and western states that are showing a great deal of growth, other opportunities exist in many states. Particularly, states that have a lot of farms and farmland near or within commuting distance to major cities offer opportunities for real estate professionals. These farms and farmland are being parceled off and sold to the highest bidder so builders can develop single-family homes in deed-restricted communities on the land. Other things to consider when contemplating relocation include job growth rate and average cost of single-family homes. For more information, consult Chapter 4, Landing Your First Job.

JOB OPPORTUNITIES FOR SALESPEOPLE AND BROKERS

Many people are needed to list and sell residential, commercial, industrial, and farmland properties. Additionally, other real estate professionals are needed to manage and lease commercial, industrial, and investment properties.

Residential Real Estate Sales Agent

Residential sales agents have what is probably the most widely known position in the real estate field. Their faces may be on billboards, in glossy magazines, and on magnets or other promotional giveaways because they are always looking for ways to gain more business. The sales agent's job revolves around contact with people.

Residential sales agents list homes for sale, and they sell homes that they or other agents have listed. While some homeowners attempt to sell their own homes, many more homeowners decide to list their homes through a real estate salesperson. This is one of the major ways residential agents earn their living—through getting new people to list their homes for sale with them. Agents usually perform a market analysis on each home they list to determine a fair selling price. They do this by carefully looking at the home to be sold for upgrades and detriments, and then comparing it to similar homes in the vicinity that have recently been sold. Once a salesperson gets a listing, he or she is guaranteed a commission when it is sold, no matter who sells it.

Another way agents earn their living is through selling homes that are currently listed for sale either by them or by another agent. First, the agent meets with potential buyers to get a sense of the type of home they want and can afford (many will "pre-qualify" their buyers at this stage by completing a form to see how much the buyers can afford to pay for a home based on income and debt figures). Then the agent consults the multiple listing service or MLS. The MLS is a complex computer network of homes for sale that have been listed by real estate sales agents or brokers, which is accessed by computer. You can plug in information you get from the buyers about the type of house they're interested in, and generate a list of properties that meet those specifications.

Agents then show buyers relevant homes, often driving them by or stopping in for a first-hand look. Computer technology has brought many changes to this stage in the process. Agents can now show many homes "virtually," via computer. Many potential buyers have already been on the Internet looking at listings before they approach an agent. Once they make a connection with a real estate office, they may have a list of homes they'd like to see. An agent in California says:

There are advantages to having clients actively involved in the search process. For one thing, they have a better sense of what the market is like when they come to you. However, their involvement keeps you on your toes. If they're surfing the Internet for listings, they expect you to also. They don't want to miss anything.

Once buyers are interested enough to make offers on properties, sales agents submit the offers to sellers, and may also deal with counter offers.

Historically, sales agents worked on behalf of the seller, not the buyer, even though they spent a good deal of time driving buyers around to look at homes. However, today many agents are now working as "buyer's agents" or performing what is called "dual agency," in which they represent both parties. It is the agent's responsibility to inform all parties to any real estate transaction what role he is playing. Many agents present their role in writing and have the buyer and seller sign it to clear up any possible confusion. The specialty of buyer's agent is becoming more prevalent; watch out for anything that relates to the topic of "agency" when you take your pre-licensure course(s). See Chapter 2 for more information about real estate courses and training programs.

Residential real estate sales agents are normally independent contractors, not employees, and they earn their living by getting commissions on the homes they list and sell. They normally do not earn salaries or get an hourly wage. Although it may be difficult in the beginning, if you have the talent, drive, and ambition, you can list and sell homes without limit. It is this potential for significant earnings that draws many people into the residential real estate sales field.

Typical Minimum Requirements

All states require that real estate salespeople become licensed before they can sell or list real estate. While requirements vary depending on what state you want to get your license in, a few standard minimum rules apply to most: you must be over 18 years old and possess a high school diploma or its equivalent (except in Missouri). You will probably be required to be affiliated with a real estate broker before you can get your real estate agent's license. Brokers own or manage the real estate office from which you'll be working as an agent. Look up your state in Chapter 3 under State Licensing Requirements for more specific information, including educational requirements, exams, and fees.

Typical Income Level

Income levels vary greatly depending on the location and the size of the real estate company and more important, the experience and talent of individual sales agents. According to the Bureau of Labor Statistics, an average annual income level for full-time real estate agents was $28,020 in 1998. People who have been in the business for many years and get a lot of repeat business and referrals from satisfied customers may make significantly more money per year.

Commission rates on the sale of a home normally range from 5 to 10%, with an average of 6%. Each commission earned by a sales agent is normally shared with the sales agent's broker, in a ratio that is mutually agreed upon when you join the company. The split is often 50:50. However, as noted above, experienced sales agents may get a much better ratio (as much as 70:30, 80:20 or more if they bring in a heavy volume of sales on a consistent basis). If you list a home and another sales agent sells it, or vice versa, then the commission is first split 50:50 between your broker and the other agent's broker. Therefore, if you list and sell the same home, your commission will be much higher than if you perform only one of these functions for any particular home.

Residential Real Estate Broker

Real estate brokers own or manage the company or franchise for which sales agents work. They often were sales agents themselves, who decided to move ahead in their careers by either going into management in a large firm, starting a franchise, or branching out and starting their own business. Brokers are often legally responsible for the work of their sales agents. The degree to which brokers are involved in the daily operations of the sales agents varies widely. Some closely supervise all of their agents, or at least the new ones.

Others continue to spend a lot of their time selling properties to bring in more commissions to the office, and leave the sales agents to fend for themselves. You'll find out more about management styles of brokers and how they impact their sales agents in Chapter 5. Brokers often manage the advertising of the homes their sales agents list, oversee general administrative duties of running an office, and may help to train new salespeople. Some sales agents get the training and license of a broker, but continue to work in sales under the auspices of another broker. These people are often called associate brokers.

Typical Minimum Requirements

As with sales agents, minimum requirements vary depending in which state you want to get a broker's license. Brokers typically need to pass a written exam, and in many states are required to attend from 50 to 90 hours or more of real estate broker training. Some states also require brokers to have from one to three years of experience as a real estate sales agent before they can apply to become a broker. However, in many cases a bachelor's degree in real estate may be substituted for the sales experience.

Typical Income Level

Brokers receive the real estate commission for each sale that their agents make, and they split that commission with the agent. The ratio is normally 50:50 for new salespeople. Many brokers will entice their best agents to stay with them by sharing more and more of the commission, sometimes going as high as 20:80 in favor of the salesperson. In certain offices, brokers let their sales agents keep 100% of their commissions—the brokers make their money by charging hefty desk fees, which may range from a few hundred dollars to well over a thousand dollars a month.

Brokers who own large real estate firms with many successful sales agents have the potential for earning a significant amount of money each year. However, brokers normally don't start out in such a good place. Many new brokers have to struggle to make ends meet and may have to log in long hours to keep the company afloat until it starts to earn significant commissions. The average annual income for full-time brokers in 1998 was $45,640, including commissions, according to the Bureau of Labor Statistics. Of course, many experienced brokers earn significantly more than that.

Commercial Real Estate Agents and Brokers

Commercial real estate agents and brokers do many of the same things residential agents and brokers do, but for different types of property. Instead of selling and listing homes, these agents and brokers are selling, listing, and leasing commercial properties. These properties may include shopping centers, apartment complexes, movie theaters, small businesses, large corporate offices, and other income producing properties.

There are considerably fewer agents and brokers specializing in commercial properties than there are in residential real estate. However, what commercial real estate lacks in volume, it makes up for in excitement, due to the complex deals that need to be negotiated. But along with the excitement and rewards that lure many newcomers into this field, comes the potential for little or no income before earning commissions. Many commercial real estate deals take nine to ten months or more to close because so many people are involved in each transaction. So you need to either have excellent credentials (such as a master's degree or two in real estate and related areas) or a good network of contacts if you want to close one or more commercial deals within your first six to twelve months in the business.

Here are some common commercial real estate areas of specialization:

- ▶ Office building sales
- ▶ Office leasing
- ▶ Retail sales
- ▶ Retail leasing
- ▶ Investment property sales
- ▶ Apartment building sales
- ▶ Hotel sales
- ▶ Restaurant sales
- ▶ Land sales
- ▶ Manufactured home parks

Typical Minimum Requirements

The minimum requirements for becoming a commercial real estate agent or broker are exactly the same as for becoming a residential agent or broker.

Therefore, technically speaking, any residential real estate sales agent or broker can sell, list, or lease commercial real estate. However, the reality is that most do not. It's a highly competitive field, and many sales agents and brokers are not interested in learning about and dealing with all the intricacies of this specialized market.

Typical Income Level

Agents and brokers who specialize in commercial real estate usually do not make as many sales as their residential counterparts, but the commissions on the few sales they do close are often quite substantial. For the second quarter of 2000, the average price for transactions involving office space reached a record high of $22 million, according to *Investment Trends Quarterly*. However, many sales agents do not earn enough commissions to pay their living expenses for at least a year. Indeed, many agents don't realize a steady and significant income for two to five years after starting their specialization. But for those agents who pay the price and make it through the first few lean years, the financial rewards can be tremendous. Many successful commercial agents and brokers may earn from $100,000 to $1,000,000 in a good year.

Industrial Real Estate Agents and Brokers

Industrial real estate agents and brokers perform tasks similar to commercial agents and brokers. The difference is that they focus on selling or leasing property that is used for industry or manufacturing, including warehouses, industrial plants, and factories. Industrial sales agents and brokers need to understand the local zoning laws and environmental regulations that apply to each property under consideration. They also need to know extensive information about the surrounding community, if the buyer plans to employ a large number of employees. How is the labor market in the area? Are there adequate resources for the employees who will live near the factory or plant? Are there appropriate forms of transportation, both to get employees and supplies to the job site and to ship out the goods once they are manufactured?

A whole new set of skills and information is needed for specializing in industrial real estate. In addition to convincing buyers that a particular property is the perfect spot for them to relocate to, you'll need to help them with the financing of the deal. If the financing doesn't go through, there is no deal, and you don't get your commission. So, just as in residential real estate where sales agents help the financing process along, you'll need to know how to help the financing process along in industrial real estate.

Typical Minimum Requirements

While any residential real estate sales agent or broker can sell, list, or lease industrial real estate since the minimum requirements for becoming an industrial real estate agent or broker are exactly the same as for becoming a residential agent or broker, most do not. It's a highly competitive, specialized field. Those in industrial real estate usually use their skills solely within their area of specialization.

Typical Income Level

Similar to commercial agents and brokers, industrial agents and brokers do not close as many sales as residential agents and brokers, but the sales they do close net them large commissions. However, since deals take so long to close in the industrial arena, sales agents and brokers often face a severe lack of earnings when first entering the field. Significant earnings can take anywhere from one to five years to achieve. You might consider phasing into this specialty once you've established yourself in the residential market.

Farm and Farmland Agents and Brokers

If your background includes living on or near a farm, you'll have a head start on specializing in farm and farmland sales. Knowing general background information about farms and farmland before you enter this area of specialization will be a big help. You'll understand the needs of your clients perhaps better than those who lack your background. However, you can study the information necessary to become a success in agricultural real estate. Be prepared to learn about:

Crop values	Climate
Tax incentive programs for farmers	Water rights

Value of farm equipment	Drainage
Value of farm animals	Minerals
Types of soil	Land leases

The first step is to gain the knowledge you need to converse with farmers and interested buyers by taking courses in farm and farmland sales. Check with your local real estate schools to see if they offer such courses. Another option is to take the course on land brokerage that is sponsored by the Realtor's Land Institute (a branch of the National Association of Realtors). See Appendix B for contact information, or log onto their web site at www.rliland.com.

Typical Minimum Requirements

The minimum requirements for listing and selling farm and farmland real estate are the same as for the residential real estate sales agent and broker. However, due to the specialized nature of the field, you'll obviously want to gain an understanding of farms and their value before branching out into this area. This is a small niche market that requires a high degree of specialization from those who choose to work in it exclusively.

Typical Income Level

Again, since sales agents and brokers who sell farms and farmland often do so in conjunction with other real estate, such as residential or commercial, their earnings are usually mixed. It may take anywhere for a year or more to close on selling a farm, but if that commission is worth $20,000 to $25,000, it can be well worth it. It's difficult to gauge a typical income level for farm and farmland sales agents because so many of them do not sell and list farms exclusively.

IS A CAREER IN REAL ESTATE RIGHT FOR YOU?

You've read the job descriptions, and heard from a number of people in the field about what it takes to be a success in real estate. Could you be one of those success stories in the future? Jot down your answers to the following questions and then take a look at what those answers mean by reading the paragraph after the quiz.

1. Do you genuinely like people?
2. Do you appreciate having variety in your workday?
3. Are you good at math?
4. Are you a self-starter?
5. Do you have good listening skills?
6. Do you like to have a high degree of security in your life?
7. Do you prefer working alone more than with other people?
8. Do you have a hard time motivating yourself to do things?
9. Do you enjoy a routine that is the same every day?
10. Do you value a high level of privacy and quiet time when you are at work?
11. Do you enjoy negotiating?
12. Do you enjoy working in a variety of environments?
13. Are you tactful and attentive to other peoples' needs?
14. Do you present yourself in a professional manner?
15. Are you good at solving problems?
16. Do you feel that weekends should be spent with your friends or family?
17. Do you dread calling people you don't know?
18. Do you get especially nervous when meeting new people?
19. Do you have trouble displaying self-confidence?
20. Do you pay close attention to details?
21. Are you extremely organized?
22. Do other people consider you friendly?
23. Do you enjoy getting involved in community events?
24. Do you enjoy meeting and talking to a variety of people?
25. Are you honest and trustworthy?

If you answered yes to the majority of questions numbered 1–5, 11–15, and 21–25, and no to the majority of questions 6–10 and 16–20, then you'll probably want to go full steam ahead toward a real estate sales agent or broker career.

However, if you answered yes to the majority of questions numbered 6–10, and 16–20, and no to the majority of questions 1–5, 11–15, and 21–25, then you may want to consider one of the related jobs in real estate. Jobs that don't center quite so squarely on selling and that provide a steady income and a more routine workday would probably better suit you—such as a mortgage broker or title searcher.

THE INSIDE TRACK

Who: Don and Bert Marcy

What: Husband-and-wife agent-broker team

Where: Coldwell Banker Schlott Realtors, Madison, New Jersey

How Long: 21 years

INSIDER'S STORY

Don came to real estate after having worked for a Wall Street firm for 15 years or so, commuting to New York City. As he approached the age of 40 he said, "If I'm going to work this hard, I'd rather work for myself than for someone else." For many years, as friends would consider buying a house, they always asked Don to come and have a look. Given this kind of pre-established credibility—and as a veteran homeowner and home renovator—Don decided to capitalize on his experience.

Bert's background was also from another field: education. Having worked 16 years as a highly popular and very well regarded classroom teacher, Bert had excellent "people" skills and a long track record as a well-organized self-starter. With young children at home, joining Don as he began his real estate career seemed ideal.

Education has been a big part of Don and Bert's success. They've taken courses in virtually every aspect of real estate, including such specialties as Property Management, New Home Sales, International Buyers, Corporate Relocation, Selling Prestigious Properties, and others. Don has even taught courses for other agents, developing seminars in Residential Renting, Writing Effective Ads, and Marketing Unusual Properties.

In the 21 years they've been working together as a team, they have been on the list of New Jersey's top salespeople every year. Since they've always worked in the town in which they live, they enjoy plenty of repeat business, from those moving to larger homes, to those relocating out of state or moving to an "empty nester" condo or town home.

INSIDER'S ADVICE

"We've seen a lot of change in this business over the years, but the basics have remained the same. First and foremost," says Don, "you have to like people and houses. And you have to enjoy being a matchmaker. The real thrill is finding the right fit. You don't have to be a 'sales' person. You need to be a good problem solver, with the ability to understand what people are really looking for. Then, you simply go out, and work like crazy to help them find it."

So, what else do they feel is involved? "Commitment," says Bert, "and a willingness to be serious about taking responsibility for someone else's hopes and dreams. This is no place for a part-timer or a dabbler," she continues. "If you're not willing to invest the time to do the job right, don't do it at all. There is too much at stake to do otherwise."

Don adds "That doesn't mean you have to make it your 40-hour-a-week job; it just means that you shouldn't try to do another job while you sell real estate too. Bert is absolutely right: You need to make a commitment."

Other traits the pair thinks are important include: absolute honesty, the ability to manage time, and a high degree of personal organization. "On this 'honesty' thing," Don says, "there is a lot we REALTOR®s have to prove, over and over again. There is a lingering perception among homebuyers that ours is a 'cut-throat' field where you have to be a real 'shark' to survive. Maybe this was true a long time ago, but today the image of the hot-shot salesman who will say anything and do anything to get the sale is as outmoded as the buggy whip."

"For success in this field, the basics have always been the same," Don claims. "Put your client's interests first, ahead of your own, and make sure that everything you do and say keeps that principle first and foremost. If you always act in your client's best interest, and you keep the REALTOR® Code of Ethics in mind, you'll always be headed in the right direction."

CHAPTER two

GETTING THE EDUCATION YOU NEED

THIS CHAPTER explains the educational opportunities available to those planning a career as a real estate professional. You'll see several real estate program descriptions from a number of schools, and learn how to evaluate training programs to find the one that best suits your needs. You'll also learn some interesting tips about financing your education. Also covered are topics such as online educational opportunities, continuing education, and professional designations.

EVERY STATE in America requires its real estate professionals to be educated in their field before they can get licensed and begin working. While requirements vary from a single course that can be completed in a weekend to college credits that are earned in a year or more, they all cover such basic information as listings and closings, financing, and contracts. There is a great deal of important information, skills, and practices you will need to know before getting your first listing or making your first sale. As Carol Shapiro, Executive Officer of the Eastern Middlesex (Massachusetts) Association of Realtors points out:

> Making mistakes in this business can be very costly. Understand all of the disclosure laws, consumer protection laws, fair housing and civil rights laws, and lending practices. Take courses in areas where you want to specialize—land, residential, commercial, and industrial, rentals, or condominiums and cooperatives.

In order to gain education beyond the basic licensing requirement, many salespeople and brokers take more courses than just those specified by their states. They may choose to earn extra certificates in specialized areas, or even work toward an associate, bachelor's, or master's degree in real estate. There are a number of ways in which to get the real estate training you need, either to fulfill the education requirement, or to begin your career with a degree in hand.

HIGH SCHOOL PREPARATION

If you haven't yet completed high school, you can take courses that will help you to prepare to enter the real estate field. First, focus on basic skills such as reading comprehension, writing, computer literacy, and mathematics. Then, take as many of the following classes as possible:

▶ Business Math
▶ Social Studies
▶ History
▶ Foreign Language
▶ Communications
▶ English
▶ Office Skills

By building a strong educational foundation while still in high school, you'll increase your chances of succeeding in the next phase of your training, whether it's a certificate, an associate degree, a bachelor's, or graduate degree.

CERTIFICATE PROGRAMS

Certificate programs, that normally cover the real estate basics you'll need to pass a licensing exam, can take anywhere from one long weekend to several months to complete. They are offered at private real estate schools (some owned by large brokerage firms, such as the Century 21 Real Estate Academy), business schools, many technical and community colleges, and some colleges and universities. If you wish to begin your career with a competitive edge, you can earn certificates in specialty areas, going beyond the basics. These areas include real estate finance, appraisal, and investment.

Like most other types of schooling, certificate programs grant certificates at the completion of the program only to those students who meet their requirements. This usually means you must have regular attendance, an academic average of a "C" or higher (2.0 GPA), and a passing score on a final test.

Course offerings from a Texas real estate certificate training program are listed below to give you an idea of what you can expect from this type of education. Note that some courses are offered on CD-ROM, so you can study at home. Texas requires its salespeople to take one of the Principles courses, both the Law of Agency and Law of Contracts courses, plus an additional 90 hours of study in core or related courses (180 hours total). For this school's program, then, the cost of pre-licensing education is approximately $900.00.

Principles of Real Estate I (30 hours)

An in-depth fundamentals course covering the state's license act, Fair Housing, listing contracts, rights in land, contracts, and much more. This class will comply with the Real Estate Commission's principles and Fair Housing requirements. CD-ROM now available. $150.00

Principles of Real Estate II (60 hours)

This course allows you to acquire core hours and fulfill the Principles and Fair Housing requirement. All the subjects in Principles I plus leases, property management, investments, closing, and title issues. (Take either I or II.) CD-ROM now available. $220.00

Law of Agency (30 hours)

Who does the agent represent? This course answers the question, along with many other legal questions. Are you familiar with the state employment laws and the Deceptive Trade Practices Act? A required course for anyone applying for a Real Estate Salesperson's license. $150.00

Law of Contracts (30 hours)

This course covers the basic residential contract and addenda, as well as basic Real Estate Finance. A required course for the salesperson's license. $150.00

Real Estate Finance (30 hours)

This course provides an overview of traditional forms of finance. It covers sources of mortgage money, conventional mortgage money programs, FHA mortgage money, Veteran's loan programs as well as how to qualify buyers. CD-ROM now available. $150.00

Residential Appraisal (30 hours)

An introduction to the appraisal process. The course includes three different approaches to determine value, plus reconciliation, data collection, site valuation, and the appraisal report. $150.00

Real Estate Investments (30 hours)

An introduction to investments in real estate covering ownership, financing of investments, taxes and feasibility studies. $150.00

Property Inspection for Agents (30 hours)

This class shows the agent how to detect property defects. Knowledge of this topic helps the agent in dealings with both buyers and sellers. The course also addresses duties and limitations of home inspectors. $150.00

Real Estate Brokerage (30 hours)

If you plan to manage or open a brokerage firm, or are currently in management, you should consider this class. It covers personnel issues, plan development, marketing, and analyzing the market. $149.00

Law (30 hours)

An excellent introduction to Real Estate Law. This course addresses subjects such as leasehold estates, landlord-tenant relationships, default, and fraud. $150.00

ASSOCIATE DEGREES

An associate degree program's length of study for full-time students is two academic or calendar years. Standard entrance requirements include a high school diploma or a GED, college preparatory courses, and entrance and placement exams. Two year Real Estate degrees are usually granted as Associate in Applied Science. While the degree is not intended for students who plan to transfer to a four-year college or university, some individual courses may be transferable. Other areas of emphasis offered in the associate of applied science degree include marketing, human resources management, legal secretary, accounting, and financial services management. Some courses in these areas may be open to those seeking a degree in real estate.

Associate degrees in real estate may be obtained at community and technical colleges, as well as at private two-year or junior colleges. You can find out the location of community colleges in your area by contacting your state's Department of Higher Education (see Appendix B), or check the worldwide web through a search engine such as *Yahoo.com* for community colleges, which are listed by state. Junior colleges are two-year institutions that are usually more expensive than community colleges because they tend to be privately owned.

JUST THE FACTS

Still in high school? You may be able to receive some college credits by enrolling as a "guest student" or auditor at your local community college. Get a copy of the school's course list, and pick out one or two you are interested in. Then, contact the admissions director. Explain your career plans and interest in sitting in on a course. You'll have to pay for it, but in many cases the credit is transferable when you enter college for a degree.

Listed below are the courses required for a real estate major in a program leading to an associate of applied science degree in real estate. The program is offered at a technical college in Wisconsin. State residents pay $2,800.00 in tuition per year.

Associate of Applied Science Degree in Real Estate Brokerage

First Semester

Course No.	Course Name		Credits
101-105	Accounting Fundamentals		3
107-102	Microcomputer Applications		3
194-101	Real Estate Fundamentals		3
194-190	Bldg Design/Structure		3
194-197	Real Estate Mathematics		3
801-195	Written Communication		3
		Total	18

Second Semester

194-125	Real Estate Records		3
194-182	Real Estate Law		3
801-196	Oral/Interpersonal Communication		3
809-158	Ethics		3
809-196	Intro to Sociology		3
809-191	Psychology of Human Relations		3
		Total	18

Third Semester

102-100	Contemporary Business		3
104-136	Sales Principles		3
194-184	Real Estate Finance		3
194-189	Real Estate Environment Issues		2
809-195	Economics		3
	Elective		3
		Total	17

Fourth Semester

102-160	Business Law I		3
194-101	Real Estate Property Listing		2
194-177	Real Estate Marketing		3
194-193	Real Estate Investments		3
	Elective		3
		Total	14
		Degree Total	67

BACHELOR'S DEGREES

Colleges and universities offer undergraduate (usually four-year) programs in which you can earn a bachelor's degree in a variety of real estate–related fields. Entrance requirements are more stringent than for community colleges; admissions personnel will expect you to have taken certain classes in high school to meet their admission standards. Your high school GPA (grade point average) and standardized test scores (most often the Scholastic Aptitude Test or SAT) will be considered. If your high school grades are weak, or it has been some time since you were last in school, you might want to consider taking courses at a community college to refresh your skills. You can always apply to the college or university as a transfer student after your academic track record has improved. You can also enroll as a "non-matriculating student," meaning that you can take courses, and even be graded and get a transcript, but you are not working toward a degree. Roberta Dinerstein, a broker for over 15 years, says:

> After I got my broker's license, I didn't want to open my own office. Instead, I chose to continue my education in real estate by taking courses in appraisal and construction at a local university. This enabled me to do appraisal work in addition to sales. So, if there is an estate for sale, or an estate in contest, I can step in and appraise it.

Be aware that state or public colleges and universities are less expensive to attend than private colleges and universities because they receive state funds to offset their operational costs. Consider too the size and quality of each school's real estate program. Colleges and universities with large, well-funded programs are better able to help you land a job once you graduate. They typically offer career-counseling services, with a network of alumni who hire recent graduates. One such school is the University of Cincinnati, which has a real estate program within its College of Business Administration. Real estate majors take courses in business (accounting, finance, information systems, management, marketing, and quantitative analysis) and real estate. They are also exposed to other disciplines that impact the field of real estate, including construction, geography, planning, and civil engineering. This is typical of bachelor's degree programs in real estate; you will be required to take only a certain number of courses directly relating to your major, and can then choose among many others to fulfill the rest of your credit requirements.

Below are course descriptions for the required real estate courses at the University of Cincinnati. Full-time, in-state tuition costs just over $6,000 per year.

Real Estate Principles

The introductory course to the real estate program designed for majors and non-majors. RE 391 is designed to introduce the student to real estate career opportunities and the field of real estate by reviewing the basic concepts of urban economics and market analysis, which affect land use, rents, and values. Economic base analysis, city growth trends, and the impact of transportation costs are reviewed. This course focuses on the housing market; buying versus renting, government policies affecting housing, the office market, and touches upon retail and industrial market trends. This is a survey course, which includes some fundamental technical skills such as an introduction to cash flow analysis, financing, geographic information systems, and valuation concepts.

Real Estate Finance

Analytical techniques for evaluating income producing property, sources of financing, loan packaging, and key financial ratios are reviewed. Investment topics include cash flow analysis, risk analysis, rate of return projections, Real Estate Investment Trusts, and capital market trends. Computer spreadsheets are used in this course.

Real Estate Appraisal

Theory and application of methods to value real property. Real estate appraisal reviews systematic methods to value residential and income producing property, influences upon market value, trends in the appraisal industry.

Real Estate Law

The nature of real property ownership rights, transfer of ownership, broker-agency relationships, land use controls and regulation are reviewed.

Real Estate Special Topics

This course focuses on different topics. Among these are research and writing skills, geographic information systems which map market data, and Internet resource utilization. Typically offered in the fall or spring quarters. See the Director of the Real Estate Program for further information.

Development Methods, Cases and Negotiation

This is the real estate integral area capstone course. Cases and negotiation exercises serve to emphasize the integration of material from several business core areas. A sample of the topics covered in some of these cases includes, but is not limited to: present value analysis and general economic feasibility, global economic trends, political risk analysis, management of risk (financial, political, economic), financing strategies and alternatives, market research interpretations and data quality assessment, management of multiple team objectives and prioritization, quantitative modeling based on prioritization to reduce complex situations.

GRADUATE DEGREES

If you already have a bachelor's degree, and are now considering a career in real estate, you may wish to pursue a graduate degree in your chosen field. Since these degrees are offered at colleges and universities, much of the information given above regarding these institutions holds true for those seeking master's degrees. While they are not common for those pursuing a job as a residential agent, master's degrees in real estate are beneficial for those with long-term career goals in advanced positions within the real estate field.

One of the many schools offering graduate programs in real estate is Cornell University, in Ithaca, New York. A master's degree is offered through the College of Architecture, Art, and Planning. As with the University of Cincinnati, Cornell's Program in Real Estate allows students to study in many disciplines, taking courses in the College of Engineering, the School of Hotel Administration, the College of Human Ecology, and the Johnson Graduate School of Management. Full-time tuition at Cornell is $23,760 per year. Below are listed the core courses required for the degree, along with many of the electives open to real estate majors.

Core Courses

Principles of Real Estate

Advanced Real Estate

Real Estate Development Process

Real Estate Marketing and Management

Real Estate Seminar Series

Real Estate Project Workshop

Planning and Managing the Workplace

Construction Planning and Operations

Public and Spatial Economics for Planners

Real Estate Law

Managerial Finance

Macroeconomics and International Trade

Statistical Methods for the Social Sciences

Elective Courses

College of Agriculture and Life Sciences

Community and Changing Property Institutions

Environmental Economics

Futures and Options Trading

International Environmental Issues

Land Economics Problems

Land Reform Old and New

Politics and Economics of Rural and Regional Development

Site Construction

Site Engineering

Urban Design and Planning: Designing Cities in the Electronic Age

College of Architecture, Art, and Planning

Building Technology, Materials, and Methods

City and Regional Planning Workshop

Environmental Controls Site Planning

Environmental Law

Historic Preservation Law

Industrial Restructuring: Implications for State and Local Policy

Local Economic Policy Field Workshop

Low-Cost Housing

Regional Planning and Development in Developing Nations

Residential Development

Seminar in Project Planning in Developing Countries

Seminar in Urban Political Economy

Urban Economics

Urban Housing Developments

Urban Public Finance

College of Arts and Sciences

Economic Problems of Latin America

Economics and the Law

The Economy of China

Environmental Economics and Policy

Japanese Ethnology

Location Theory and Regional Analysis

Public Finance: Resource Allocation and Fiscal Policy

College of Engineering

Project Management

School of Hotel Administration

Advanced Development and Construction

Hospitality Real Estate Finance

Housing and Feeding the Homeless

International Development

Real Estate Law

Services Marketing

Strategic Marketing

College of Human Ecology

Applied Public Finance

Household and Family Demography

Housing and Society

Housing Economics

Housing for the Elderly

Housing, Neighborhood and Community

Human Factors: The Ambient Environment

Introduction to Building Technology

Introduction to Human Environment Relations

Programming Methods in Design

Seminar on Facility Planning and Management

Urban Economics and Policy

Johnson Graduate School of Management

Corporate Financial Policy

Economic Evaluation of Capital Investment Projects

Entrepreneurship and Enterprise

Entrepreneurship Lab

Financial Markets and Institutions

International Finance

Investments and Portfolio Analysis

Judgment and Negotiations

DISTANCE TRAINING PROGRAMS

In the certificate training program outlined on page 27, you may have noticed that some courses were available on CD-ROM. This represents a growing trend in education, including not only certificate programs, but associate and even bachelor's degrees as well. Hundreds of colleges and universities offer programs with names like Degrees at a Distance, Correspondence Courses, or Long Distance Learning, that allow you to study and take courses on your own, without attending formal classes. These programs are designed so students may earn a degree while working full- or part-time, or who have other commitments that make it difficult for them to commit to a rigid class schedule.

Distance learning is independent study. It focuses on the idea that adults, through their jobs, personal activities, and general life experience, have many of the tools necessary to be successful, independent learners. Generally, they have organizational and time management skills, basic writing and communication skills, motivation and initiative, and the willingness to make serious commitments to their education. If you already have some work and life experience behind you, and believe you are a good candidate for independent study, this could be an excellent way to get the real estate education you need. It may also be a good option for working real estate professionals to complete their associate or bachelor's degrees, or to get additional training.

As mentioned above, one option for distance training is using CD-ROMs or other computer software that you can purchase and use at home when it is convenient for you. Another option is Internet courses, in which you get lessons and tests to download on your home computer. You can then e-mail questions, assignments, and tests back to the school. This option's advantage is that you have some contact with an instructor or other qualified person at the institution giving the course. Log onto the National Realtor's Association site www.erealtoruniversity.com to take a class demonstration, giving you an idea of what it's like to take an online course. At the New York State Association of Realtors website, www.nysar.com/realtor_university.html, see some of the hundreds of courses available to both pre-licensees and licensed real estate professionals. To find more sites, search the Internet with keywords such as "real estate online education."

If you've already chosen a school, ask if they offer any real estate distance learning programs. You should also contact your state's real estate commission, licensing law office, or appraisal board (listed in Appendix B) to find out if self-study courses are an option for you to fulfill the pre-licensing or continuing education requirements. You can check Appendix A to find names of books that offer additional information about distance learning programs.

HOW TO CHOOSE A PROGRAM

Whether you are looking for a certificate program, or seeking a degree from a college or university, there are a number of things you will need to consider before you select a school. Begin by developing a clear picture of what you want from your education, and what your needs are. For instance, if you need to work full-time while getting your real estate education, you will need to consider schools that offer flexibility, such as classes on nights and weekends. If you plan to live at home while pursuing your education, then location must be a priority. Once you know what you want and need from a school, you can begin to research the schools themselves.

You might begin by reading Appendix C, which offers a directory of schools offering real estate training programs, including certificate programs. You can find more schools by searching the Internet using key words such as "real estate training" and "real estate education." Keep in mind during your search that, like salespeople and brokers, schools must also be licensed as real estate "professionals" by your state, and you will receive credit only for certificates earned through licensed schools. To find out which schools and programs are licensed, check your state's Real Estate Commission or Board's website, or call them to request a list.

Certificate Programs

There are a number of variables to consider when looking at the certificate programs offered in your area. Some programs offer "intensive" courses which take only a few days to complete, while others require a few hours a week for two or three months. Costs vary widely from school to school. Request brochures, log onto each school's website, and call schools to speak with the director or an instructor to learn even more. Questions you should ask include those about:

▶ Requirements for admission
▶ Class schedule (are night and weekend classes offered, or daytime only?)

► Costs
► Types of certificates offered
► Home study
► Length of the program
► Exam success rate (How many of those who pass the certificate course go on to pass the licensing exam on the first try?)

Associate, Bachelor's, and Graduate Degrees

As with choosing a certificate program, you should get as much information about each two-year school as possible, and then weigh the information against your needs. For example, if you plan to live at home while earning a two-year degree, you can consider only those schools within easy commuting distance. If you will work full-time while in school, you can consider only those schools offering the classes you need to take on nights and weekends. If you plan to enter the real estate field as a broker, look at schools that offer a degree in real estate brokerage.

To find junior or two-year colleges that offer the education you seek, check the Internet using the keywords "two year college," or use a search site such as Yahoo.com, which has junior colleges listed by state in its Education section. From there, search for schools offering real estate programs.

When looking for a college or university, there are many things to consider. Will you live at home and commute, or are you willing to relocate and live on or near a campus farther from home? Do you need to work while in school, or will you attend full-time? Do you want a general degree in real estate, where you can take courses in a variety of related topics, or do you want to specialize in an area such as property management or appraisal? Get a clear picture of what you want from a school before looking at your options. Once you know what you want, begin your search for a school that offers it.

Below are listed many resources to help you with your search. Note that there are both websites and books that can help you through each step of the process, from finding the right school, to applying and getting accepted.

Online College Guides

Most of these sites offer similar information, including various search methods, the ability to apply to many schools online, financial aid and scholarship information, and online test taking (PSAT, SAT, etc.). Some offer advice in selecting schools, give virtual campus tours, and help you decide what classes to take in high school. It is well worth it to visit several of them.

www.embark.com—a good general site

www.collegequest.com—run by Peterson's, a well-known publisher of college guide
    books (they can also be found at www.petersons.com)

www.review.com—a service of *The Princeton Review*. Plenty of "insider information" on
    schools, custom searches for school, pointers on improving standardized test scores

www.collegenet.com—on the web since 1995, best for applying to schools online

www.collegereview.com—offers good general information, plus virtual campus tours

www.theadmissionsoffice.com—answers your questions about the application process,
    how to improve your chances of getting accepted, when to take tests

College Guidebooks

Two Year Colleges 2001

Peterson's Guides, 2000.

    The best-selling authority on two-year colleges.

The Fiske Guide to Colleges 2000

Edward B. Fiske, with Robert Logue. Crown Publishing Group, 1999.

    Fiske is the former education editor of the *New York Times*. His guide focuses on the "best and most interesting" 300+ colleges and universities. They are selected on the basis of their academic strength. Also included is a list of "best buys."

Barron's Profiles of American Colleges
(with Windows and Mac software)

College Division of Barron's Educational Series, 1998.

    This book rates every accredited four-year college and university in the United States. It includes an Index of Majors, so you can zero in on those schools offering the program you want, plus software that guides you through the preparation of admission forms and letters.

The Insider's Guide to the Colleges

The Staff of the *Yale Daily News*. St. Martin's Press, Inc., 1999.

The most frank of the guides, and the only one researched and written by current college students. There are no statistics, course descriptions, or other "dry" information. What you will find is student-to-student advice on the admissions process, how to choose a school, and how to pay for your education, and portraits of the schools that cover many aspects of life on campus, including the condition of the dorms, and the dating scene.

VISITING COLLEGES AND UNIVERSITIES

If possible, take the time to visit the schools you are interested in, and speak with a guidance counselor or other school representative at each one. These counselors are trained to help you identify your needs and decide if their school will meet those needs. Follow these steps when preparing for an on-campus visit:

- ▶ Contact the office of admissions (or the school administrator) to request an appointment to visit. Remember to ask for the name of the person making the appointment and the person you will be meeting with. Try to schedule a meeting with an instructor in the real estate program as well as a guidance counselor in the admissions or counseling department, if available.
- ▶ Carry with you a copy of your high school transcript and record of any completed college courses if you will have the opportunity to meet with an admission counselor during your visit.
- ▶ Create and bring with you a list of honors or awards you have received in high school, another career field, or the in community.
- ▶ Read the school's promotional brochures and other printed material, and make a list of questions not answered in it.

Asking the Right Questions

When choosing a four-year or graduate program, you should visit several schools and narrow your choices down to two or three schools. The next step when applying to any program—whether two- or four-year, or graduate—is to ask tough questions about each program so you can make the final selection. Here are some of those questions. After each, you'll find the answers you should listen for, as well as other important considerations.

1. What requirements will I need to attend?

    Check with each school that you are considering to learn its specific entrance requirements. Requirements vary from school to school. For instance, you may be required to do any one or more of the following:

    ▶ Take English, math, or science placement tests
    ▶ Take and achieve a certain score on the SAT or ACT if you have not already taken them in high school
    ▶ Have a certain level GPA from high school
    ▶ Provide proof of immunization
    ▶ Write a personal essay stating why you are seeking admission
    ▶ Provide the names and phone numbers for three or more personal references

2. What are the qualifications of the faculty?

    There should be some faculty members with advanced degrees (M.A., M.S., M.B.A., Ph.D.) or faculty members who have extensive experience as real estate professionals and instructors. In a four-year college or university, you can expect the majority of professors to hold advanced degrees. In shorter programs, such as a certificate program or individual courses, you'll find more instructors who are currently practicing as real estate professionals. In all types of schools, however, the faculty should be accessible to students for individual conferences or meetings when necessary.

3. Is the school accredited?

    It's important that the school you choose be accredited. Accreditation is a rigorous and complex process that ensures sound educational and ethical business practices at the schools that achieve accreditation. It's a process schools undergo voluntarily.

    Accrediting agencies are either national or regional. The name of the accrediting agency for the school you're interested in will probably be plainly printed on the school's general catalog because most schools are proud of their accredited status. If you can't locate the information in a school's printed materials, call the school and ask for the name(s) of its accrediting agency or agencies. Note that financial aid offered through government programs is not available to students at non-accredited schools. See Appendix B for contact information for several national and regional accrediting agencies.

4. What will the program cost?

Tuition varies according to many factors but especially according to the length of the program and the area in which the school is located. Often, tuition costs also depend on if you are a resident of the state in which you are applying for school. You should take some time to figure out how much each program that you are considering will cost. If the tuition is not listed in the college's course catalog or on their website, call the school and ask. Remember to add the following items when figuring out total cost: books, admission fees, lab fees, rent (or room and board), transportation, and child care.

5. Can I get tuition reimbursement for this program?

Some real estate schools offer you a list of sponsoring real estate companies that are willing to reimburse you for costs of the real estate course if you agree to sign on with their company as a salesperson. Often, the reimbursement will take place after you close your first sale.

6. What is the student–teacher ratio?

The student–teacher ratio is a statistic that shows the average number of students assigned to one teacher in a classroom. It's important that the ratio not be too high. Education suffers if classrooms are too crowded, or if a teacher has too many students to be able to see everyone who wishes to be seen for a private conference. According to one of the top national accrediting agencies, the Accrediting Council for Independent Colleges and Schools (ACICS), a reasonable student–teacher ratio for skills training is 30 students to one teacher in a lecture setting and 15 students to one teacher in a laboratory or clinical instruction setting. At very good schools the ratio is even better than the ACICS recommends.

7. When are classes scheduled?

Find out if the school you're considering offers any weekend or evening classes. If you are working full-time during regular business hours while attending school, you'll need to find a school that offers classes at non-traditional times.

8. Is the campus environment suitable?

When you visit the school, determine how the campus feels to you. Is it too big? Too small? Too quiet? Is the campus in a bustling city or rural community? Is it easily accessible? Do you need to rely on public transportation to get there? Select a school that has a campus environment that meets your needs.

9. Does the school offer child care facilities?

If this is an area of concern, you'll want to tour the child care facilities and interview the people who work in the child care center to see if the care is suitable for your children.

Application Tips from Admissions Directors

■ Apply as early as you can. You'll need to fill out an application and submit high school or GED transcripts and any copies of SAT, ACT, or other test scores used for admission. If you haven't taken these tests, you may have to before you can be admitted. Call the school and find out when the next program starts, then apply at least a month or two prior to make sure you can complete requirements before the program begins.

■ You may receive a pre-written request for high school transcripts from the admissions office when you get your application. Make sure you send those requests as soon as possible, so the admissions process is not held up in any way.

■ Make an appointment as soon as possible to take any placement tests that may be required.

■ Pay your fees before the deadline. Enrollment is not complete each quarter or semester until you have paid all fees by the date specified on your registration form. If fees are not paid by the deadline, your classes may be canceled. If you are going to receive financial aid, apply as early as you can.

■ Find out if you must pass a physical or provide any medical history forms such as immunization records early in the application process, so this does not hold up your admission.

FINANCING YOUR TRAINING

You can qualify for aid at several different types of schools, including community colleges, technical colleges, universities, and vocational schools that offer short-term training programs, certificates, associate degrees, and bachelor's degrees. You can often qualify for some type of financial aid even if you're attending only part-time. The financial aid you'll get may be less than in full-time programs, but it can still be worthwhile and help you pay for a portion of your real estate training program.

Before diving into the world of financial aid, you should first determine if your employer will reimburse you for the cost of your training. While this option may not be available in every state or for every real estate career, it's definitely worth exploring.

Tuition Reimbursement for Salespeople

What better form of financial aid could you find than getting your entire tuition for a training program reimbursed? It does sound enticing, but there may be a catch, often in the form of a job offer that is written in cement. That is, a particular real estate company reimburses you the cost of a real estate sales course if you agree to work for that company for a set number of months or until you close your first sale. While not all real estate companies offer this benefit, this route can be a good way to finance your training if you are willing to commit to working for the company.

One way to find real estate companies that are willing to reimburse you for the basic pre-licensing real estate courses is from the real estate schools that you are considering attending. Some schools will provide prospective students with a list of real estate companies that offer tuition reimbursement to people who agree to work for them. Keep in mind that these offers are usually only geared toward short-term real estate courses that satisfy the pre-licensing education requirement in your state—not the lengthier real estate associate or bachelor's degree programs. If you are planning to get an associate or bachelor's degree, it may make more sense for you to enroll in your program of study and take the pre-licensing education courses there, so you can get college credit for them. If you do enroll in an associate or bachelor's degree program, a whole new world of financial aid will open up to you.

Federal Financial Aid

To receive federal financial aid from an accredited college or institution's student aid program, you must:

► Have a high school diploma or a General Education Development (GED) certificate, pass a test approved by the U.S. Department of Education, or meet other standards your state establishes that are approved by the U.S. Department of Education.
► Be enrolled or accepted for enrollment as a regular student working toward a degree or certificate in an eligible program.
► Be a U.S. citizen or eligible non-citizen possessing a Social Security number. Refer to Immigration and Naturalization Service (INS) in the section entitled *Resources* that appears at the end of this chapter if you are not a U.S. citizen and are unsure of your eligibility.
► Have a valid Social Security number.
► Make satisfactory academic progress.
► Sign a statement of educational purpose and a certification statement on overpayment and default.
► Register with Selective Service, if required.
► Have financial need, except for some loan and other aid programs.

To apply for federal financial aid you must complete the Free Application for Federal Student Aid (FAFSA). You can complete the form even if you haven't yet been accepted or enrolled in a school. However, you do need to be enrolled in an accredited training program in order to actually receive any funds from a federal financial aid program. You can get this form from several sources: your public library, your school's financial aid office, online at www.finaid.org/finaid.html, or by calling 1-800-4-FED-AID. You need to get an original form to mail in; photocopies of federal forms are not acceptable. The FAFSA determines your eligibility status for all grants and loans provided by federal or state governments and certain college or institution aid, so it is the first step in the financial aid process, and it should be done as soon as possible.

Apply for financial aid as soon as possible after January 1 of the year in which you want to enroll in school. For example, if you want to begin school in the fall of 2002, then you should apply for financial aid as soon as possible after January 1, 2002. In addition to federal financial aid—including grants and student loans—you can also investigate your eligibility for the many scholarships that have been established to benefit students for a variety of reasons.

Scholarships

Scholarships are often awarded for academic merit or for special characteristics (for example, ethnic heritage, interests, sports, parents' career, college major, geographic location), but some are also based on financial need. Unlike student loans, scholarships do not need to be paid back. You can obtain scholarships from federal, state, school, and private sources.

The best way to find scholarship money is to use one of the free search tools available on the Internet. After entering the appropriate information about yourself, a search takes place that ends with a list of those prizes for which you are eligible. Try www.fastasp.org, which bills itself as the world's largest and oldest private sector scholarship database. www.collegescholar ships.com and www.gripvision.com are also good sites for conducting searches. If you don't have easy access to the Internet, or want to expand your search, college financial aid officers also have plenty of information about available scholarship money.

If you're currently employed, check to see if your employer has aid funds available. Also check with the real estate or business department at the school you plan to attend to see if they maintain a bulletin board or other method of posting available scholarships that are specific to real estate programs. Here are a few examples of real estate scholarships for which you might be eligible.

▶ **Appraisal Institute Education Trust Scholarship Fund**
The Appraisal Institute Education Trust Scholarship Fund offers scholarships of between $2,000–3,000 to undergraduates and graduate

students who major in real estate, land economics, or real estate appraisal. For more information, contact the Director of Scholarships, Appraisal Institute Education Trust Scholarship Fund, 875 N. Michigan Avenue, Suite #2400, Chicago, IL 60611; the phone number is 312-335-4100.

▶ **California Association of REALTORS® Scholarship**

The California Association of REALTORS® Scholarship Foundation awards scholarships to undergraduate students studying for a career in real estate. This scholarship is an academic–based scholarship, however awards will first be given to students who demonstrate financial need. The two award categories give up to $2,000 to students of four-year colleges/universities, and up to $1,000 to students of two-year colleges and to seniors enrolled in their last semester of high school. Students must have successfully completed at least 30 units. To apply for this scholarship, contact the California Association of Realtors, 525 S. Virgil Avenue, Los Angeles, CA 90020; the phone number is 213-739-8200.

▶ **George M. Brooker Collegiate Scholarship for Minorities**

Each year, two undergraduates and one graduate student of real estate will receive tuition assistance ($1,000 per undergraduate and $2,500 per graduate student) from the George M. Brooker Collegiate Scholarship for Minorities program that is affiliated with the Institute of Real Estate Management (IREM). The deadline for the fall semester is March 1 of the same year. For more information, contact the IREM Foundation Coordinator, 430 N. Michigan Avenue, Chicago, IL 60611-4090; the phone number is 312-329-6008.

▶ **Paul H. Rittle, Sr. Memorial Scholarship**

Primary attention is placed on financial need and a demonstrated commitment to a career in real estate management for the Paul H. Rittle Sr. Memorial Scholarship. Awards are made on a course-by-course basis for students taking courses from the Institute of Real Estate Management (IREM). You may receive more than one scholarship, but only one in a given calendar year. The scholarships may reach a maximum of $2,000 for Certified Property Manager (CPM) membership qualification courses and $500 for IREM's Accredited Resident Manager (ARM) qualification courses. The deadlines to apply for this scholarship are March 1 and August 1. To apply for this scholarship, contact: IREM Foundation Coordinator, 430 N. Michigan Avenue, Chicago, IL 60611-4090; the phone number is 312-329-6008.

▶ **Real Estate Endowment Fund Scholarship**

The Real Estate Endowment Fund offers scholarships to real estate majors of up to $800 per academic year for low income/disadvantaged students in California. Students must be enrolled at least half-time and have a minimum GPA of 2.0. You can apply for this scholarship by obtaining an application from the Real Estate Department Coordinator or the Financial Aid Office at your community college.

The scholarships mentioned above are only a small sample of the many scholarships for which you might be eligible. Also the above introduction to the financial aid options available to you is necessarily abbreviated and should only serve as a starting point. Regardless of the length of the training you are pursuing, be sure to explore all the avenues for financial aid that are available to you and never assume that you will have to finance your training in its entirety out of your own pocket.

CONTINUING EDUCATION

Once you've begun your career in real estate, you will need to keep informed about changing laws, technology, and other factors that may impact the way you do your job. Continuing education is one way in which you can get the information you need. In fact, most states have made it a requirement for license renewal (a process you will need to go through every one to two years, depending on the state you're licensed in). As with pre-license education, there are many opportunities to get continuing education credits online. Courses are also offered at the same state-licensed schools that offer pre-license education.

Bert Marcy, a realtor in New Jersey for over 20 years, says:

Today's real estate professional needs to keep on learning. Most brokerage companies provide continuing courses to help agents keep their skills current in areas such as technology, negotiation, legal and fair housing issues, and many other areas. And other courses are available from local and state real estate organizations. There is always something new. And even if you think you've mastered the old stuff, it is worthwhile to review the basic skills too.

In Louisiana, agents and brokers must get eight hours of continuing education credits each year, while in Kansas, they must complete 12 hours every two years. Oregon requires its agents and brokers to complete 30 hours of continuing education every two years. At least 15 hours must be in required topics, which include:

Trust Accounts
Agency
Misrepresentation
Commercial Brokerage and Leasing
Fair Housing
Land
Anti-Trust
Property Management
Contracts
Rule and Law Update
Evaluation of Property
Brokerage Management
Real Estate Taxation: Federal, State, and Local

You also may be able to fulfill your state's requirement by taking courses at the college level, perhaps in an area of real estate specialization, such as assessment or property management. For more information on your state's requirements, as well as a list of licensed schools and course listings, check out your state's Real Estate Board or Commission's web site, listed in Chapter 3.

JUST THE FACTS

As of this book's publication date, New Jersey is the only state that does not have a continuing education requirement for real estate professionals. While the New Jersey Real Estate Commission is currently involved in discussions on the issue, no formal rules or other legislation has been drafted. New Jersey does, however, have a pre-licensing education requirement.

PROFESSIONAL DESIGNATIONS

Real estate education can be used to distinguish yourself once you've begun your career. Different from continuing education credits, which are licensing necessities in almost every state, professional designations, offered through the National Association of Realtors (NAR), are earned voluntarily. (For more information about the NAR, see Chapter 5.) And while many of the courses offered in designation programs may be used for continuing education credits, when taken together and successfully completed by a professional who is an active member of the NAR, they lead to the awarding of a designation.

IN THE NEWS

The National Association of REALTORS® (NAR) asserts that realtors with a designation earn almost $20,000 more, annually than their counterparts without a designation.

The four most popular designations are detailed below, including the Graduate Realtor Institute (GRI), the Accredited Buyer Representative (ABR), the Certified International Property Specialist (CIPS), and e-PRO. Course descriptions are based on NAR's promotional material.

GRI: Graduate Realtor Institute

To earn the designation, REALTORS must take all eight GRI courses, totaling 90 hours in credit and pass each course exam with a 70% or above. Candidates have five years to complete the course work and once they have done so can use the GRI letters, following their names to demonstrate their achievement.

RI 401—Delivering Effective Real Estate Services to Today's Consumer
RI 402—Real Estate Legal Issues…Not Knowing Can be Dangerous
RI 403—Financing for Today's Home Buyer
RI 404—Real Estate Investment and Taxation Issues
RI 405—Residential Construction, Home Inspection, ADA, Land Use, and Environmental Hazards
RI 406—Pricing and Evaluating Residential Properties
RI 407—Building Your Real Estate Practice
RI 408—Using Technology to Grow Your Business—The Complete Automation Program for Real Estate Professionals

ABR: Accredited Buyer Representative

To earn the ABR, you must complete the 15-hour ABR course and pass the exam with an 80% or better. You must also demonstrate your acting as a buyer's representative in five documented transactions within an 18-month time span and be a member in good standing of your Association of REALTORS®. Two letters of recommendation from buyer clients and Real Estate Buyer's Agent Council (REBAC) members are also required. When you register for the ABR course, you also receive one full year's membership in the Real Estate Buyer's Agent Council.

The ABR course covers the proper techniques and practices of buyer representation that will enhance your bottom line. It clarifies agency relationships, presents negotiation strategies, explains the advantages of buyer representation from the buyer's, seller's, and the listing and selling broker's perspectives and it also identifies sources of buyer clients. This course may be taken online at REALTOR® University.

CIPS: Certified International Property Specialist

If you want to do more business in expanding markets, even global markets, this designation is for you. For real estate professionals interested in dealing effectively with real estate clients from diverse cultures and countries, you'll learn how to capture the growing market and discover how to put available resources to work for you.

To earn the CIPS designation, qualified individuals must declare their candidacy, and within two years complete and pass with a 70% all four CIPS courses, plus the Essentials prerequisite course. They must also document client/customer representation in at least three international transactions, complete the CIPS application, and pay all required fees.

Essentials of International Real Estate
The America's and International Real Estate
Europe and International Real Estate
Asia/Pacific and International Real Estate

e-PRO Internet Professional

NAR's newest certification course is taken entirely online, and students are given six months to complete it. The e-PRO Certification curriculum can be completed in 12–20 hours, with additional time required to complete interactive assignments. By design, the course will teach the REALTOR® about Internet business principles including:

Operational: How to streamline real estate operations to save time and money, and gain a strategic advantage over competitors.
Marketing: How to generate new business by using all the tools of the Net. Emphasis is on online-specific marketing skills as ways to connect with nameless, faceless consumers.
Protocol: How to create and maintain profitable relationships with the new, Internet empowered consumer. Understanding and implementing

these protocol principles offers some of the most potent facets of e-PRO Certification.

Standards & Behavior: How to avoid the six areas of online risk: legal, regulatory, tort liability, online business goodwill, operations, and security. Based upon material by Michael J. Russer, author of the industry's first set of Internet Policies and Procedures, and strategic advisor to the Association of Real Estate License Law Officials (ARELLO).

Positioning: How to stay on top of the innovation curve without losing one's mind. Identify, evaluate, and implement new Internet business models.

This chapter has covered the many types of training available to those working in real estate, and to those planning to enter the field. As with many other professions, your success may be directly related to how well educated and informed you are. Because of state requirements, plan to acquire more education on an annual basis after you are licensed. Technology is rapidly changing, and you'll want to learn how to stay on top of the changes and apply this new technology to your career. The courses you are required to take, as well as any you voluntarily sign up for, will not only enhance your business, but also help to keep you on the cutting edge of your career.

THE INSIDE TRACK

Who: Carol Shapiro

What: Executive Officer of the Eastern Middlesex
           Association of REALTORS®

Where: Reading, Massachusetts

How long: Five years as Executive Officer; 14 years as broker and
           owner of Carol Marrano Real Estate, Ltd.

INSIDER'S STORY

I earned my real estate broker's license in October of 1977, while a single mother of two young boys. Within two and a half years, I opened my own company, which I ran for the next 14 years. During this time, I took many courses to learn business acumen as well as selling techniques. I also became president of the Eastern Middlesex Association of

REALTORS®, and helped to create the continuing education bylaw for our association. At the time, Massachusetts was one of only two states in the nation without a continuing education requirement.

As a volunteer, I served as Chairperson of the Massachusetts Association of REALTORS® Community Service Committee, the Communications Committee, and the Charitable and Education Foundation (which I helped to create). I was also President of the Eastern Middlesex Association of REALTORS® Women's Council.

In my current position, I helped to establish the Eastern Middlesex Real Estate Academy. Our school offers continuing education courses, real estate licensing courses, and computer training for REALTORS®.

INSIDER'S ADVICE

My advice for those considering the real estate profession is, first, plan to work full time. It is very frustrating and difficult for salespeople to try to earn a decent income on a part time basis. Second, you should expect to work on evenings and weekends, as this is when homebuyers are generally available to view properties. You owe it to your family, your friends, and yourself to make a schedule that includes personal as well as professional time.

I would also advise you to join the REALTOR® organizations so you can receive the latest information regarding legislation affecting property rights, and all the necessary tools to conduct your business in a lawful, knowledgeable manner. Get as much education as you can, too. Being educated is the best way to avoid making costly mistakes. There are so many laws affecting the sale and purchase of real estate; if you don't know them, you may violate one and end up involved in a lawsuit.

CHAPTER three

LICENSING

ONCE YOU'VE looked into the career options in real estate, and learned about the training you'll need to enter the profession, your next step is to consider licensing. In order to sell or appraise real estate in any state in the country, you need a license. This chapter will help you to understand licensing requirements, showing the similarities and differences between the 50 states. It will also guide you to the agencies that handle real estate licensing across the United States.

EVERY STATE has laws and regulations governing the purchase, sale, and appraisal of real estate. These laws and regulations also determine how interested persons can become real estate professionals.

REAL ESTATE LICENSING REQUIREMENTS

Although the requirements vary from state to state, they have many similarities. For instance, most states require that you be at least 18 years of age, and have a high school diploma or GED to become a salesperson. It is mandatory in many states that you be a resident when you apply for a license. As discussed in Chapter 2, every state has educational requirements for salespeople, brokers, and appraisers, as well as an exam that must be passed, before a license is issued. Many states also require that agents carry liability insurance to protect them in the event of a lawsuit. Below, we'll discuss some of these requirements in detail.

Good Character

Those states requiring "good character" of their real estate professionals want to be sure that licensees are trustworthy enough to handle large sums of their clients' money. In order to determine character, they may ask for recommendations, conduct background investigations (including finger-printing), or ask your employer to sign a certificate. Many states decline applications from those who admit to certain felony convictions. For instance, in Vermont, the Real Estate Commission will not consider any-one who has been convicted of a crime involving forgery, embezzlement, obtaining money under false pretenses, conspiring to fraud, or any crimi-nal or civil offense which contains an element of fraud. They also refuse licenses to those who have been convicted of violating the Real Estate Broker's Act.

JUST THE FACTS

Some states, such as New Jersey, require license applicants to furnish their social secu-rity numbers. This information is used to determine if the applicant is behind on child support payments or is the subject of a child support warrant. If there is a warrant, or the applicant is six months or more in arrears on payments, the license application is rejected. If such a child support situation occurs after licensing, the state can revoke the license.

Many states also look at people's past histories involving real estate licens-es, denying licenses to those who have been denied licenses previously, or had a license suspended or revoked in any state. In North Carolina, licens-es may not be issued to those who have had license applications denied in another state. Some states, however, take applications from those with felony convictions or other legal setbacks, but they are reviewed individually, and then accepted or denied on a case-by-case basis.

Liability Insurance

It is a requirement in many states for licensees to be covered by liability insurance. Some states mandate coverage under an Errors and Omissions policy, which is issued by an insurance company much like homeowner's and automobile liability insurance. Errors and Omissions policies may be taken out by individuals or by companies (covering their employees). Some employers require their employees to pay for their own coverage, others split the cost of the policy with their employees, and others pay in full for coverage as a benefit to their employees. One company's current rate was $830 per year for $1,000,000 of coverage.

Another type of liability coverage is called Recovery or Guaranty Funds. These funds are created by collecting money from every licensee in a state, and then pooling it. If a licensee has a judgment against him or her, it is paid out of the pool. For states using these funds, licensees must participate in the program. The amount they must contribute varies, as does the amount of coverage. For instance, some states charge each licensee $20.00 per year, which gives them $100,000 in liability coverage.

Licensing Exams

Exams for most states are given by national testing services. The most popular are Applied Measurement Professionals (AMP) of Lenexa, Kansas; Assessment Systems, Inc., (ASI) of Philadelphia; Experior Assessments of Salt Lake City, Utah; and PSI Examination Services of Glendale, California. If your state uses one of these services, you will need to contact the service directly to register, usually after your application has been approved.

To prepare for the exam, which includes both a general test and a state specific test, most testing services offer downloadable study materials, as well as practice exams, on their websites. You can also prepare using the online real estate practice tests for each state offered on LearnATest.com. To learn more about these practice tests visit www.learnatest.com's real estate site. The testing services' websites also include test schedules, with times, dates, and locations, as well as applications that can be filled out online. Check the list below for contact information for the four largest testing services. Some states still prefer to create and administer their own tests. For more specific information, including test locations, course requirements, and exam outlines, check out each state's website, or call the office directly. We have included the contact information you will need below.

Real Estate Licensing Exam Testing Services

Applied Measurement Professionals (AMP)

8310 Nieman Road

Lenexa, KS 66214

913-541-0400

www.applmeapro.com

Alabama, Georgia, Illinois, Michigan, Missouri, Montana, Nebraska, Nevada, North Dakota, South Dakota, Washington, and Wyoming

Assessment Systems, Inc.

c/o Webmaster

3 Bala Plaza West, Suite 300

Bala Cynwyd, PA 19004

888-204-6231

www.asisvcs.com

Alaska, Arkansas, Colorado, Delaware, Florida, Hawaii, Indiana, Kansas, Kentucky, Massachusetts, Minnesota, New Jersey, Rhode Island, Tennessee, and Utah

Experior Assessments

254 South 600 East

Salt Lake City, Utah 84102

800-326-3926

www.experioronline.com

Arizona, Idaho, New Hampshire, New Mexico, Ohio, Pennsylvania, South Carolina, and Texas

PSI Examination Services

100 West Broadway, Suite 1100

Glendale, CA 91210

800-733-9267

www.psiexams.com

Connecticut, Iowa, Louisiana, Maryland, Michigan, North Carolina, Vermont, and

Wisconsin

JUST THE FACTS

ARELLO, the Association of Real Estate License Law Officials, publishes a newsletter six times a year called *Boundaries*. It deals with the ever-changing laws and regulations affecting the real estate field. You don't have to be a licensed agent or broker to subscribe. For information on the newsletter, and the organization in general, log onto their web site: www.arello.org.

STATE LICENSING AGENCIES AND THEIR REQUIREMENTS FOR AGENTS AND BROKERS

ALABAMA

Real Estate Commission

1201 Carmichael Way

Montgomery, AL 38106

334-242-5544

www.arec.state.al.us

General Requirements: at least 18 years of age (salesperson), 19 (broker); U.S. citizen and resident of Alabama; good character; no real estate license rejected or revoked in any state within the past two years; Errors and Omissions insurance. Brokers' License applicants must show proof of at least two years of full-time, licensed salesperson experience.

Education Requirements: 60-hour salesperson course, plus a three-hour post-license course to receive permanent license; 60-hour broker course.

Exam: AMP

Fees: License $75.00 (salesperson), $95.00 (broker); Exam $75.00

ALASKA

Division of Occupational Licensing

Real Estate Commission

3801 C Street, Suite 722

Anchorage, AL 99503

907-269-8162

www.dced.state.ak.us/occ/prec.htm

General Requirements: at least 19 years of age; employed by a broker (if applying for salesperson's license); if convicted of a felony, must have completed the sentence; not be under indictment for forgery, theft, extortion, conspiracy to defraud, or any other felony implying character untrustworthiness; apply for license within six months of passing exam. Broker applicants must show proof of at least 24 months of full-time salesperson experience; must own a real estate business or work as the broker at a corporation or partnership; if convicted of a felony, must be at least seven years since serving of sentence.

Education Requirements: 20 classroom hours for salespersons, with an additional 15 hours for broker training.

Exam: ASI

Fees: Application $50.00, Licensing $300.00, Surety $30.00

ARIZONA

Department of Real Estate

2910 North 44th Street, Suite 100

Phoenix, AZ 85018

602-468-1414

www.re.state.az.us

General Requirements: at least 18 years of age; good character; the applicant has had no real estate license denied within one year or revoked within two years of application; brokers must also show proof of three years of licensed broker or salesperson experience.

Education Requirements: 90 hours of Real Estate Principles and Practices, plus a six-hour Contract Law and Contract Writing for salespersons (work experience may be substituted; determined on a case-by-case basis).

Exam: Experior Assessments

Fees: License $94.00 (salesperson), $169.00 (broker); Exam $85.00 (salesperson), $115.00 (broker)

ARKANSAS

Real Estate Commission

612 South Summit Street

Little Rock, AK 72201-4740

501-682-2732

www.state.ar.us/arec/arecweb.html

General Requirements: at least 18 years of age; Errors and Omissions insurance; brokers must show proof of two years of licensed salesperson experience.

Education Requirements: 60 hours of real estate education for salespeople, 30 of which must be in Basic Principles of Real Estate.

Exam: ASI; required of salespeople and brokers

Fees: Application, $50.00, License $50.00 (salesperson), $70.00 (broker); Exam $70.00; Recovery fund $25.00

CALIFORNIA

Department of Real Estate

2201 Broadway

Sacramento, CA 95818

916-227-0931

www.dre.cahwnet.gov

General Requirements: at least 18 years of age; good character; U.S. citizen or resident alien; brokers must show proof of at least one year of experience as a licensed salesperson, or have educational equivalent, and show proof of current employment.

Education Requirements: one college-level course in Real Estate Principles for salespeople; brokers must take eight college-level courses, including Real Estate Practice, Legal Aspects of Real Estate, Real Estate Finance, Real Estate Appraisal, Real Estate Economics or General Accounting, and three real estate electives.

Exam: administered by the Department of Real Estate; preparation materials are given to applicants after successfully completing the education requirement.

Fees: License $87.00 (salesperson), $142.00 (broker); Exam $60.00 (salesperson), $95.00 (broker)

COLORADO

Department of Regulatory Agencies

Division of Real Estate

1900 Grant Street, Suite 600

Denver, CO 80203

303-894-2166

www.dora.state.co.us/Real-Estate

General Requirements: at least 18 years of age, good character; brokers must have two years of experience and present a statement from their current employing broker.

Education Requirements: for both Associate Brokers (entry-level position) and Independent Brokers (those with salesperson experience): 48 hours in Real Estate Law and Practice, 48 hours in Colorado Contracts and Regulations, eight hours in Trust Accounts and Record Keeping, 24 hours in Real Estate Closings, 32 hours in Practical Applications.

Exam: ASI

Fees: License $155.00; Exam $74.00

CONNECTICUT

Department of Consumer Protection

Real Estate Division

165 Capital Avenue

Hartford, CT 06106

203-566-5130

www.dcp/state/ct/us/licensing/realestate.htm

General Requirements: good character, determined by three letters of recommendation; brokers need two years of salesperson experience.

Education Requirements: Real Estate Principles and Practice (30 hours) for salespeople and brokers; Real Estate Appraisal (30 hours) and Real Estate Elective (30 hours) or more than two years of experience for brokers.

Exam: PSI; taken after application is approved and all other requirements are met

Fees: License $40.00 (salesperson), $60.00 (broker); Exam $65.00; Real Estate Guaranty Fund $20.00 (affords $25,000.00 liability coverage)

DELAWARE

Real Estate Commission

861 Silver Lake Boulevard, Suite 203

Dover, DE 19904-2467

302-739-4522, ext. 219

www.state.de.us/research/profreg/realcomm.htm

General Requirements: at least 18 years of age; good character; broker applicants must have five years of active, licensed experience, and a list of at least 30 sales or other qualified transactions.

Education Requirements: Real Estate Practice (99 hours, salespeople); Real Estate Practice plus Broker course (99 + 90 hours, brokers).

Exam: ASI

Fees: Exam $85.00; Real Estate Guaranty Fund $25.00 (affords $25,000.00 liability coverage)

FLORIDA

Division of Real Estate

400 West Robinson Street

Orlando, FL 32801

407-423-6053

www.state.fl.us/dbpr/re/index.shtml

General Requirements: good character (fingerprinting); brokers must show proof of one year of experience as an active, licensed salesperson.

Education: Pre-Licensing Course I (63 hours) for salespeople; Pre-Licensing Course II (72 hours) for brokers.

Exam: ASI; Salesperson or Real Estate law exam; must be authorized to take exam

Fees: License $144.00 (salesperson), $154.00 (broker); Exam $45.50

GEORGIA

Real Estate Commission

Suite 1000—International Tower

229 Peachtree Street, NW

Atlanta, GA 30303-1605

404-656-3916

www2.state.ga.us/Ga.Real_Estate/

General Requirements: at least 18 (salesperson) or 21 (broker) years of age; good character; broker applicants must show proof of three years of licensed experience.

Education Requirements: 75-hour Real Estate Licensing course, or 2 college-level real estate courses at a college or university for salespeople; 60-hour Real Estate Brokers' course, or 3 college-level real estate courses at a college or university for brokers.

Exam: AMP; once enrolled in pre-licensing course, candidate can apply for the exam and a license; exam is taken after passing the course.

Fees: License (four years) $165.00 (salesperson), $235.00 (broker); Exam $68.00

HAWAII

Real Estate Commission

250 South King Street, Room 702

Honolulu, HI 96813

808-586-2643

www.state.hi.us/hirec

General Requirements: at least 18 years of age; U.S. citizen or resident alien; good character; broker applicants must have active Hawaii salesperson license and three years of experience.

Education Requirements: pre-license course (may be waived if applicant has college degree in real estate, law school degree, active license in state with similar or superior education requirement, or at least four college-level real estate courses).

Exam: ASI; license application given out at test site to those who pass exam.

Fees: License $50.00; Exam $68.00

IDAHO

Real Estate Commission

P.O. Box 83720

Boise, ID 83720-0077

208-334-3285

www.2.state.id.us/irec

General Requirements: at least 18 years of age; high school diploma or GED; good character; Error and Omissions Insurance; broker applicants must have at least two years of active experience, or more than the required level of education.

Education Requirements: Essentials of Real Estate and Real Estate Practices (45 hours each; salespeople); Brokerage Management, Real Estate Law, and two electives (90 hours total, brokers).

Exam: Experior Assessments; take before applying for license

Fees: License $254.00; Exam $65.00

ILLINOIS

Office of Banks and Real Estate

Attention: Real Estate Division

500 East Monroe, Suite 200

Springfield, IL 62701

217-782-3414

www.obre.state.il.us/REALEST

General Requirements: at least 21 years of age, or 18 years of age with 48 hours toward education requirement; high school diploma or GED; broker applicants need sponsor card from employer (may be issued to self if self-employed).

Education Requirements: Real Estate Transactions (45 hour course) or bachelor's or master's degree in real estate, accounting, law, finance, business, or other approved degree (salespeople); Real Estate Transactions, Brokerage Administration, Contracts and Conveyances, Appraisal, Sales and Brokerage, Real Property Insurance (120 hours total) or bachelor's degree including real estate courses (broker).

Exam: AMP; license application given out at test site to those who pass

Fees: License $100.00; Exam $49.00

INDIANA

Real Estate Commission

302 West Washington Street

Indianapolis, IN 46204-2700

317-232-2980

www.state.in.us/pla/realestate/index.html

General Requirements: at least 18 years of age; good character; sworn certificate from employing broker certifying current employment; broker applicants must have one year of active, licensed experience.

Education Requirements: salespeople must pass a 40-hour course covering Indiana License Law and Professional Standards; Law of Agency; Contracts; Interests in Real Property; Evidence of Title; Deeds; Legal Property Descriptions; Mathematics; Taxes; Valuation of Real Property; Financing; Listing Contracts and Purchase Agreements; Settlement Procedures; Property Management, Government Regulations; Planning and Zoning; brokers must pass a 24-hour course including Indiana License Law and Professional Standards; Law of Agency; Contracts; Financing; Settlement Procedures; Escrow Responsibility; Recordkeeping; Government Regulations; Appraising.

Exam: ASI

Fees: License $25.00 (salesperson), $50.00 (broker)

IOWA

Professional Licensing & Regulation Division

Real Estate Division

1918 SE Hulsizer Avenue

Ankeny, IA 50021

515-281-3183

www.state.ia.us/government/com/prof/realesta/realesta.htm

General Requirements: at least 18 years of age, sponsorship by employing broker, Errors and Omissions insurance; broker applicants need at least two years of experience.

Education Requirements: salespeople must pass a 60-hour pre-license course covering: Introduction to Real Estate; Iowa License Law; Ownership, Encumbrances, Legal Descriptions; Transfer of Title and Closing; Contracts; Agency and Antitrust; Valuation, Finance, and Real Estate math; Property Management/Leasing; Fair Housing, Environmental Risks, and Health Issues. Brokers must pass a 72-hour course, with eight hours each of Contract Law and Contract Writing; Iowa Real Estate Trust Accounts; Principles of Appraising and Market Analysis; Real Estate Law and Agency Law; Real Estate Finance; Federal and State Laws Affecting Iowa Practice; Real Estate Office Organization; Real Estate Office Administration; Human Resources Management.

Exam: PSI

Fees: License $75.00 (salesperson), $120.00 (broker); Exam $91.00

KANSAS

Real Estate Commission

Three Townsite Plaza, Suite 200

120 SE 6th Avenue

Topeka, KS 66603-3511

785-296-3411

www.ink.org/public/krec

General Requirements: at least 18 years of age; high school diploma or GED; salesperson applicant must prove association with a hiring broker who can attest to good character; broker must have two years of experience.

Education Requirements: 30-hour Principles of Real Estate course for sales-people; 24-hour Broker's Pre-License Course for brokers (may be done through home study).

Exam: ASI

Fees: License $25.00 (salesperson), $150.00 (broker); Exam $75.00

KENTUCKY

Real Estate Commission

10200 Linn Station Road, Suite 201

Louisville, KY 40223

502-425-4273

www.krec.net

General Requirements: at least 18 years of age; high school diploma or GED; good character; broker applicants need two years of active, licensed experience.

Education Requirements: salespeople need 96 hours of real estate courses, or two college-level real estate courses; brokers need 336 hours (including salesperson requirement) in real estate courses, or seven college-level courses with at least four in real estate.

Exam: ASI

Fees: License $55.00 (salesperson), $80.00 (broker); transcript review $10.00; Exam $75.00

LOUISIANA

Real Estate Commission

P.O. Box 14785

Baton Rouge, LA 70898-4785

800-821-4529

www.lrec.state.la.us

General Requirements: at least 18 years of age; high school diploma or GED; Errors and Omissions insurance; good character; salesperson applicants must be sponsored by a licensed broker; broker applicants must have at least two years of active, licensed, experience.

Education Requirements: salesperson applicants must pass 90 hours of coursework in: Prinicples and Practices of Real Estate, Louisiana Real Estate License Law of Agency, Commission Rules and Regulations, Civil Law Pertaining to Real Estate; broker applicants must pass 150 hours of course-work in: Louisiana Real Estate License Law, Commission Rules and Regulations, Civil Law Pertaining to Real Estate, and Broker Responsibility.

Exam: PSI; applicant must be pre-approved before registering

Fees: License $45.00 (salesperson), $120.00 (broker); Exam $75.00

MAINE

Department of Professional and Financial Regulation

Office of Licensing and Registration

35 State House Station

Augusta, ME 04333

207-624-8521

www.state.me.us/pfr/olr

General Requirements: at least 18 years of age; high school diploma or GED; broker applicants need at least one year of experience and two years (60 cred-its) in a business degree program with at least 12 credits in real estate courses.

Education Requirements: salesperson applicants can either take and pass Introduction to Real Estate Course, or pass the exam without the course; broker applicants must pass a Role of the Designated Broker course.

Exam: for salespeople only, who have not taken and passed the Introduction to Real Estate course

Fees: License $100.00; Exam $100.00

MARYLAND

Real Estate Commission

500 North Calvert Street

Baltimore, MD 21202

410-230-6230

www.dllr.state.md.us/license/real_est/reintro/.html

General Requirements: at least 18 years of age; good character; salesperson applicants must be affiliated with a licensed broker; broker applicants must have at least three years of experience as a salesperson.

Education Requirements: courses must be passed before one can register for the exam; 60-hour salesperson course on Principles and Practices of Real Estate; 135 hours of broker courses.

Exam: PSI

Fees: License $45.00 (salesperson), $95.00 (broker); Exam $46.00; Guaranty Fund $20.00

MASSACHUSETTS

Real Estate Board

239 Causeway Street, Suite 500

Boston, MA 02114

617-727-2373

www.state.ma.us/reg/boards/re/default.htm

General Requirements: at least 18 years of age; good character; broker applicants must have one year of active experience as a salesperson; brokers may be interviewed by Real Estate Board; brokers need $5,000.00 surety bond.

Education Requirements: 24 hours of salesperson courses; brokers must take salesperson courses plus an additional 30 hours of broker courses.

Exam: ASI

Fees: License $55.00 (salesperson), $70.00 (broker); Exam $92.00 (salesperson), $100.00 (broker)

MICHIGAN

Department of Commerce

BOPR—Office of Commercial Services

P.O. Box 30243

Lansing, MI 48909

517-373-0490

www.cis.state.mi.us/bcs/re/home.htm

General Requirements: at least 18 years of age; good character; at least three years of experience as a licensed, active salesperson (broker applicants); salesperson applicants must be sponsored by a broker.

Education Requirements: 40 hours in real estate fundamentals (salesperson); 90 hours of approved coursework (brokers).

Exam: AMP

Fees: License $23.00 (salesperson), $38.00 (broker)

MINNESOTA

Department of Commerce

133 East 7th Street

St. Paul, MN 55101

651-296-6694

www.commerce.state.mn.us/

General Requirements: two years of experience as a salesperson for broker applicants; broker applicants must open and maintain an interest-bearing trust account; salesperson applicants must have sponsoring broker.

Education Requirements: 90 hours of approved courses (salesperson); salesperson requirement plus 30 hours of approved broker coursework (brokers).

Exam: ASI

Fees: License $145.00; Exam $67.00

MISSISSIPPI

Real Estate Commission

5176 Keele Street

P.O. Box 12685

Jackson, MS 39236-2685

601-987-3969

General Requirements: at least 18 years of age (salesperson), or 21 years of age (broker); good character; high school diploma or GED; errors and omissions insurance; resident of Mississippi; broker applicants must have at least one year of experience as a salesperson.

Education Requirements: salesperson: 60 hours of approved real estate courses; brokers: 120 hours of approved real estate courses.

Exam: Mississippi Real Estate Commission

Fees: license: $120.00 (salesperson), $150.00 (broker)

MISSOURI

Real Estate Commission

3605 Missouri Boulevard

P.O. Box 1339

Jefferson City, MO 65102

314-751-2628

www.ecodev.state.mo.us/pr/restate/

General Requirements: good character; at least 18 years of age.

Education Requirements: salesperson and broker pre-licensing courses at approved schools.

Exam: AMP

Fees: License $40.00 (salesperson), $80.00 (broker); Exam $47.00

MONTANA

Board of Realty Regulation

111 North Jackson

Helena, MT 59601

406-444-2961

www.com.state.mt.us/License/

General Requirements: at least 18 years of age; high school diploma or GED; broker applicants must have at least two years of salesperson experience, with at least 30 residential transactions, or 10 commercial, agricultural, or farm and ranch transactions.

Education Requirements: 60 hours of real estate courses.

Exam: AMP

Fees: License $200.00 if applying in an even year, $100.00 if applying in an odd year; Recovery fund $35.00

NEBRASKA

Real Estate Commission

1200 N Street, Suite 402

Lincoln, NE 68508

402-471-2004

www.nol.org/home/NREC/index.htm

General Requirements: at least 19 years of age; high school diploma or GED; salesperson applicants must have letter from sponsoring broker; broker applicants must have two years of experience; Errors and Omissions insurance.

Education Requirements: 60 hours of approved courses (salesperson); 180 hours of approved courses (broker).

Exam: AMP

Fees: License $75.00 (salesperson), $100.00 (broker)

NEVADA

Nevada Department of Business & Industry

Real Estate Division

788 Fairview Drive, Suite 200

Carson City, NV 89701-5453

775-687-4280

www.state.nv.us/b&i/red/

General Requirements: at least 18 years of age; good character (background investigation and fingerprinting); broker applicants must have at least two years of salesperson experience.

Education Requirements: salesperson: 90 hours or six semester units of instruction in Real Estate Principles, Practices, and Law (law must include a minimum of 18 hours of Nevada real estate law); brokers: 64 semester college-level units comprised of: three units Real Estate Principles, three units Real Estate Law, three units Real Estate Appraisal; 15 units in Business, Economics, or real estate related courses and 40 units in any college-level course (experience may be used as substitute for some units).

Exam: AMP

Fees: License $130.00 (salesperson), $170.00 (broker); Recovery fund and education research $40.00

NEW HAMPSHIRE

Real Estate Commission

State House Annex, Room 434

25 Capital Street

Concord, NH 03301

603-271-6658

www.state.nh.us/nhrec/license.html

General Requirements: anyone who passes exam and fulfills education requirement (brokers only) can apply for a license.

Education Requirements: 60 hours of approved pre-licensing education for brokers.

Exam: AMP

Fees: License $55.00 (salesperson), $75.00 (broker); Exam $65.00

NEW JERSEY

Real Estate Commission

20 West State Street

CN-328

Trenton, NJ 08625

809-292-8280

www.naic.org/nj/rec_lic.htm

General Requirements: at least 18 years of age; high school diploma or GED; brokers must have three years of experience as a licensed salesperson.

Education Requirements: salesperson: 75-hour salesperson general course; broker: 150 hours, including a 90-hour broker general course, 30 hours in Agency/Ethics, and 30 hours in Office Management or related topics.

Exam: ASI

Fees: License (two years) $100.00 (salesperson), $160.00 (broker)

NEW MEXICO

Real Estate Commission

1650 University Boulevard, NE, Suite 490

Albuquerque, NM 87102

505-841-9120

General Requirements: at least 18 years of age; legal resident of the U.S.; broker applicants must have two years of licensed, active salesperson experience (may be waived if education requirement is exceeded).

Education Requirements: brokers: Real Estate Law (30 hours), Real Estate Practice (30 hours), Real Estate Finance or Appraisal (30 hours); salespeople: Real Estate Law (30 hours) and Real Estate Practice (30 hours).

Exam: Experior Assessments

Fees: License (three years) $180.00; Exam $60.00

NEW YORK

Department of State
Division of Licensing Services
84 Holland Avenue
Albany, NY 12208
518-474-2651
www.dos.state.ny.us/lcns/realest.html

General Requirements: at least 18 years of age; salesperson applicants must have sponsoring broker; good character; child support statement (may not be four months or more in arrears); broker applicants must have one year of experience as a salesperson, or two years of general real estate experience (buying or selling own property, property management, etc.).

Education Requirements: 45-hour salesperson course; 45 hour broker course (brokers must also take salesperson course).

Exam: New York Department of State

Fees: License $50.00 (salesperson), $150.00 (broker); Exam $15.00

NORTH CAROLINA

Real Estate Commission
1313 Navaho Drive
P.O. Box 17100
Raleigh, NC 27619-7100
919-875-3700
www.ncrec.state.nc.us/

General Requirements: at least 18 years of age; good character.

Education Requirements: 67-hour Fundamentals of Real Estate course (salesperson); broker applicants must fulfill salesperson requirement and successfully take 60-hour broker prelicensing course (if already licensed as a North Carolina salesperson, need only take broker course).

Exam: PSI

Fees: License $30.00; Exam $58.00

NORTH DAKOTA

Real Estate Commission

314 East Thayer Avenue

P.O. Box 727

Bismarck, ND 58502-0727

701-328-9749

General Requirements: at least 18 years of age; good character; broker applicants must have at least two years of salesperson experience.

Education Requirements: 30-hour salesperson prelicensing course; 90 hour broker prelicensing course.

Exam: AMP

Fees: Exam $125.00

OHIO

Division of Real Estate

77 South High Street, 20th Floor

Columbus, OH 43266-0547

614-488-4100

www.con.state.oh.us/odoc/real

General Requirements: good character; at least 18 years of age; salesperson applicants must be sponsored by an Ohio broker; high school diploma or GED; broker applicants must have at least two years of salesperson experience with at least 20 real estate transactions.

Education Requirements: (all must be completed at a two- or four-year college or university) salesperson: Real Estate Principles and Practices (30 hours), Ohio Real Estate Law (30 hours), Real Estate Appraisal (30 hours), Real Estate Finance (30 hours); broker: same as salesperson if licensed as salesperson prior to 1984; if licensed after 1984, must complete above 120 hours plus Financial Management (30 hours), Human Resource or Personnel Management (30 hours), Applied Business Economics (30 hours), and Business Law (30 hours).

Exam: Experior Assessments

Fees: Exam $49.00 (salesperson), $69.00 (broker)

OKLAHOMA

Real Estate Commission

4040 North Lincoln Boulevard, Suite 100

Oklahoma City, OK 73105

405-521-3387

www.state.ok.us/~orec/

General Requirements: salesperson applicants must be affiliated with a licensed broker and be at least 18 years of age; broker applicants must have at least two years of active, licensed experience as a salesperson; good character.

Education Requirements: courses must be passed before one can register for the exam; 45 hours of approved courses for salespeople; brokers must complete 75 hours of advanced, approved courses.

Exam: AMP

Fees: License $200.00; Exam $46.00; Guaranty Fund $20.00

OREGON

Real Estate Agency

1177 Center Street NE

Salem, OR 97301-2505

Fax: 503-373-7153

bbs.chemek.cc.or.us/public/orea/licenses.htm

General Requirements: at least 18 years of age; background check; brokers must have three years of experience as salesperson in Oregon.

Education Requirements: salesperson: 30-hour courses in Real Estate Practice, Oregon Real Estate Law, and Real Estate Finance (or pass exams in each subject); broker: 30-hour courses in Real Estate Practice, Oregon Real Estate Law, Real Estate Finance, Real Estate Office Management and Supervision of Sales Personnel, and Real Estate Property Management (or pass exams in each subject).

Exam: Oregon Real Estate Agency

Fees: Application fee $40.00; License $180.00 (salesperson), $230.00 (broker); Exam $70.00

PENNSYLVANIA

Real Estate Commission

P.O. Box 2649

Harrisburg, PA 17105-2649

717-783-3658

General Requirements: at least 18 years old (salesperson) or 21 years old (broker); brokers must have three years of experience as a salesperson.

Education Requirements: salesperson: four college credits or 60 hours total from the following courses: Real Estate Fundamentals (30 hours) and Real Estate Practice (30 hours), waived if have BA degree in Real Estate; broker: 16 credits or 240 hours of real estate instruction.

Exam: Experior Assessments

Fees: Exam $25.00

RHODE ISLAND

Department of Business Regulation

Real Estate

233 Richmond Street, Suite 230

Providence, RI 02903-4230

401-222-2255

www.dbr.state.ri.us/

General Requirements: at least 18 years of age; good character; salesperson applicants must have sponsoring broker; broker applicants must have one year of experience as a sales agent (or fulfill education requirement).

Education Requirements: broker applicants only: 90 hours of Fundamentals of Real Estate I, II, III (or one year of salesperson experience).

Exam: ASI

Fees: Application $10.00; Exam $70.00; Recovery Fund $25.00; License (two years) $80.00 (salesperson), $120.00 (broker)

SOUTH CAROLINA

Department of Labor Licensing & Regulation

Real Estate Commission

P.O. Box 11847

Columbia, SC 29211-1847

803-896-4400

www.llr.state.sc.us/POL/RealEstateCommission/

General Requirements: at least 18 years of age for salespeople and 21 years of age for brokers; high school diploma or GED; three years of experience for brokers.

Education Requirements: 90-hour Fundamentals of Real Estate course (salespeople); same 90 hours plus 60 hours of education in advanced real estate topics for brokers.

Exam: Experior Assessments

Fees: License $75.00 (salesperson) $150.00 (broker); $10.00 credit report fee; Exam $63.00

SOUTH DAKOTA

Real Estate Commission

118 West Capitol

Pierre, SD 57501-0490

605-773-3600

www.state.sd.us/dcr/realestate

General Requirements: salesperson applicants must be affiliated with a licensed broker and be at least 18 years of age; broker applicants must have at least two years of active, licensed experience as a salesperson; good character.

Education Requirements: courses must be passed before one can register for the exam; 60-hour salesperson course on Principles and Practices of Real Estate; brokers must complete salesperson course plus 40-hour Broker Course II and 15-hour Broker Course III.

Exam: AMP

Fees: License $200.00; Exam $46.00

TENNESSEE

Real Estate Commission

500 James Robertson Parkway

Suite 180, Volunteer Plaza

Nashville, TN 37243-1151

615-741-2273

General Requirements: good character; at least 18 years of age; three years
of experience for brokers.

Education Requirement: 60 hours in Real Estate Principles and
Fundamentals; 120 hours of broker courses, including 30 hours in
Office/Brokerage Management.

Exam: ASI

Fees: Exam $60.00

TEXAS

Real Estate Commission

P.O. Box 12188

Austin, TX 78711-2188

512-459-6544

www.trec.state.tx.us/

General Requirements: at least 18 years of age; a U.S. citizen and a resident
of Texas (nonresidents may apply for special license); salesperson applicants must have a sponsoring broker.

Education Requirements: 80 classroom hours of education, 90 hours from
core real estate corses with a minimum of 30 hours of Principles of Real
Estate, three hours of Fair Housing, and 30 hours of Law Agency.

Exam: Experior Assessments

Fees: License $50.00 (salesperson), $75.00 (broker); Exam $35.00

UTAH

Department of Commerce

Division of Real Estate

P.O. Box 146711

Salt Lake City, UT 84114-6711

801-530-6747

www.state.ut.us/

General Requirements: good character; at least 18 years of age; three years of experience for broker applicants.

Education Requirements: Real Estate Principals and Practices and Utah Real Estate License Law (90 hours, salespeople); brokers must complete 120 hours of instruction in Broker Management, Advanced Appraisal, Advanced Finance, and Advanced Real Estate Law.

Exam: ASI

Fees: License $100.00; Recovery Fund $1.00; Fingerprint Processing $39.00

VERMONT

Real Estate Commission

109 State Street

Montpelier, VT 05609-1106

802-828-3228

www.vtprofessionals.org/real_estate/

General Requirements: at least 18 years of age; good character; salesperson applicants must have sponsoring broker; broker applicants must have one year of salesperson experience with at least six closed transactions, or equivalent education.

Education Requirements: brokers only, eight-hour prelicensing broker course.

Exam: PSI

Fees: License $50.00; Exam $55.00

VIRGINIA

Department of Professional & Occupational Regulation

3600 West Broad Street

Richmond, VA 23230-4917

804-367-8526

www.state.va.us/dpor/indexne.html

General Requirements: good character; at least 18 years of age; broker applicants must have three years of experience as a licensed salesperson.

Education Requirements: 60-hour Principles and Practices of Real Estate (salespeople); Principles and Practices plus 45-hour broker course (brokers).

Exam: PSI

Fees: License (includes recovery fund assessment) $95.00 (salesperson), $105.00 (broker); Exam $60.50

WASHINGTON

Department of Licensing

Real Estate Program

P.O. Box 9015

Olympia, WA 98507-9015

360-753-2250

www.wa.gov/dol/bpd/refront.htm

General Requirements: at least 18 years of age; high school diploma or GED (brokers only); broker applicants need at least two years of experience as a full-time salesperson.

Education Requirements: 60-hour course in Real Estate Fundamentals and 30-hour course in Real Estate Practices (salespeople); brokers must take four 30-hour courses in: Brokerage Management, Real Estate Law, Business Management, and one elective.

Exam: AMP

Fees: License $116.25 (salesperson), $180.00 (broker); Application and Exam $138.25

WEST VIRGINIA

Real Estate Commission

1033 Quarrier Street, Suite 400

Charleston, WV 25301-2315

304-558-3555

www.state.wv.us/wvrec

General Requirements: at least 18 years of age; high school diploma or GED; good character; U.S. citizen and resident of West Virginia; salesperson applicants must have sponsoring broker; broker applicants must have two years of experience as a salesperson, and establish a trust account.

Education Requirements: 30 hours in Real Estate Principles and Practice, 20 hours in Real Estate Law, 20 hours in Real Estate Finance, 20 hours in Real Estate Appraisal (salesperson); brokers must fulfill salesperson requirement, and take an additional 90 hours in the same subjects, with more in-depth coverage.

Exam: West Virginia Real Estate Commission (prelicensing schools give students study materials)

Fees: License $40.00 (salesperson), $80.00 (broker); Exam $25.00

WISCONSIN

Bureau of Direct Licensing and Real Estate

Department of Regulation and Licensing

1400 East Washington Avenue

P.O. Box 8935

Madison, WI 53708

badger.state.wi.us/agencies/drl/

General Requirements: good character; salespeople must have sponsoring broker; broker applicants must have salesperson license or have passed salesperson exam.

Education Requirements: 72 hours of approved salesperson courses; brokers must complete salesperson requirement, plus 36 hours in brokers' Business Management.

Exam: PSI

Fees: License $44.00, Exam $95.00

WYOMING

Real Estate Commission

2020 Carey Avenue, Suite 100

Cheyenne, WY 82002-0180

307-777-7141

realestate.state.wy.us/

General Requirements: at least 18 years of age; good character; broker applicants must have two years of experience as a salesperson; salesperson must have sponsoring broker.

Education Requirements: 30 hours for salespeople and 60 hours for brokers in Real Estate Principles, Real Estate Law, Real Estate Finance, and related topics.

Exam: AMP

Fees: License $75.00; Recovery fund $20.00; Exam $95.00

THE INSIDE TRACK

Who: Lydia Wisloski

What: Licensed REALTOR®

Where: Century 21 Advantage, Essex, Vermont

How Long: Three years

INSIDER'S STORY

When I was growing up, I wanted to be an architect. But at that time, it wasn't considered a suitable career for women, so I was encouraged to become a teacher instead. When I moved to Vermont from Pennsylvania, and bought my first house, I saw the real estate field and became interested in it. I couldn't find a teaching job right away, so I decided to take some real estate courses, mainly out of curiosity, rather than as a career step. But, I was given the opportunity to work as an agent in a small office near my home, and took the job.

I left real estate after a few years because of the demands of my family. There was too much conflict between my work and home schedules. However, I kept my license, and when I became an "empty nester," I rejoined the real estate ranks. Now, I work for a local franchise of an international company, and love the constant challenge of each transaction. Every property, homeowner, and buyer is so unique. Although there are some frustrations, my interest remains high because of the problem solving and people-oriented nature of my job.

There have been many changes in the real estate profession over the past two decades. One of these has been the refocusing to larger offices rather than a number of smaller ones. Fifteen years ago, a principal broker might have five or six offices throughout a region, trying to capture as much business as possible. Now, with the high cost of office space, the speed at which listings are sold, the expense of technology, and the ever-increasing legal issues, it is smarter for the broker to consolidate, and maintain one large office for all of her agents.

The technology is also a challenge for salespeople. There are advances being made all the time, and if you can't keep up, you will lose business. One of the advantages of working for a large franchise is that we get trained in and use the latest computer programs and other technology. But, the agents have to do their part, too; most set up home offices with computers, voice mail, and other systems that help them receive and send information; plus, they make a commitment to learning new and better ways of doing business.

INSIDER'S ADVICE

If you're thinking about entering the real estate field, I suggest that you shadow a realtor for a month. Follow this person throughout their day-to-day business, and ask plenty of questions. This is probably the best way to really understand what the profession is all about.

You should also be prepared to make sacrifices in your personal life. Real estate can eat up all of your time if you don't manage it well. Some agents choose to work as a team, and others hire assistants who help them with their workload. Take some time for yourself, with the understanding that you may lose some business while doing so. It's important to have balance in your life.

CHAPTER four

LANDING YOUR FIRST JOB

IN THIS chapter, you'll find out how to get employed once you've completed your real estate education and received your license. You'll learn where and how to look for a job, including tips on getting the most from online resources. Job search topics such as resume and cover letter writing, and the interview process, are covered in detail. We will also discuss the very real financial considerations you should address during your job search. Finally, you'll find out how to wrap up the job search process by evaluating the offers you receive, and taking your first job.

YOU'VE MADE the decision to have a career in real estate, and learned how to prepare for it. Now, how do you land a job in this exciting field? The good news is that most real estate offices continually recruit new sales agents to join their ranks. It's relatively inexpensive for them to do so, since salespeople are independent contractors (basically considered self-employed) who usually receive no benefits. Plus, the office gets a percentage of all agents' commissions, so it makes sense to have a large workforce. In addition, the turnover of sales agents is high in many real estate offices, so desk space becomes available on a regular basis.

The first step toward employment is determining where to look for a job. Consider location first, and then the type of real estate office that best matches your needs. Below, we'll discuss these considerations at length.

LOCATION, LOCATION, LOCATION

Most experts agree that you should capitalize on your knowledge of your local area by joining a company close to where you live. If you've lived there for at least a year, you probably know about the neighborhoods, schools, and other selling points, which you can then pass on to prospective buyers. However, your current location may not provide you with the opportunity for the growth and income you desire. If this is the case, or you are planning to relocate for some other reason, investigate areas that could provide you with more favorable conditions.

For instance, take a look at the areas of the country that have the highest job growth rate; these are the cities and towns experiencing economic booms. New housing is being sold, and existing homes are turning over as people move to these areas for employment in large numbers. Below is a current list of the top ten areas with their job growth averages.

City or Town	Job Growth Rate
Sarasota, Florida	7.7%
Bradenton, Florida	7.7%
Las Vegas, Nevada	7.6%
Henderson, Nevada	7.6%
Champaign, Illinois	7.3%
Colorado Springs, Colorado	7.3%
Dover, Delaware	6.9%
Dennis, Massachusetts	6.8%
El Paso, Texas	6.4%
Charleston, South Carolina	6.3%

If you are considering relocation, you might also want to look at the areas of the United States in which housing prices are highest. For each listing or sale, you will receive a larger commission. These areas may also be recommended because they are consistently desirable places to live; the housing markets thrive, and prices soar because large numbers of people seek to live there. Listed on the following chart are the five cities or towns with the highest average cost of a 2,000 square-foot home. (In comparison are the five cities or towns where the lowest average cost of a 2,000 square-foot home is just over $100,000.00.)

City or Town	Average cost of a 2,000 square-foot home
Atherton, California	$900,000.00
New York, New York	$820,000.00
Menlo Park, California	$700,000.00
Palo Alto, California	$700,000.00
Long Beach, New York	$680,000.00

JUST THE FACTS

According to the U.S. Housing and Urban Development Department (HUD), 67.7% of Americans owned their own homes in 2000. This figure represents 71.6 million home-owners, a record high.

TYPES OF REAL ESTATE OFFICES

Even if you narrow your list down to the real estate offices in your own neighborhood, you may still have several to choose from. Therefore, you'll want to visit some real estate companies to get a better feel for the ones in which you'd be most comfortable working. Several different types of real estate companies exist. Let's take a closer look at the most common types: national franchises, large independent firms, and small independent firms.

National Franchises

You have probably heard and seen a lot of advertising for national real estate franchises. They focus on building brand-name loyalty and national (or even international) recognition among the buying and selling public, and then pass along that name recognition to each independently owned and operated real estate franchise that uses their name. Franchises are buying up independent firms at a brisk rate all around the country. The franchise company licenses their name to the franchisee in return for a percentage of that firm's profits.

One of the benefits of joining a national franchise real estate company is the training they offer. These companies normally sponsor educational programs to help new sales agents become successful and to give experienced agents more advanced selling tips and techniques. They also provide the state-required continuing education classes free to their agents and brokers, at locations that are convenient to—or even in—their offices. A broker/owner from Fort Wayne, Indiana says he decided to go with a franchise because of the training and national recognition they offer:

> I've been in this business a long time, and I've seen many independent companies giving up their independence to join one of the several successful national franchises. I guess that was always in the back of my mind as I gathered information about my options. I know I made the right choice because we are doing great financially and my agents are among the most professional in the business. We take full advantage of all the training opportunities, and I do believe that the training has played a major role in helping our new agents to succeed.

Advertising, as mentioned above, is also considered a primary benefit of working for a franchise. The parent company has millions of dollars available to promote its name in many ways. Beyond the typical print, radio, and television ads, there is now sponsorship of sporting events and the Internet, both of which can increase name recognition and revenue. All of the large franchise websites allow searches of their nationwide listings. If you see an interesting property, you are then directed to a local franchise. Some large companies claim to provide hundreds of thousands of leads to their franchises in this way.

Franchised offices tend to be more structured than independent offices. This means agents may be required to attend regular sales meetings, remain in the office for scheduled "floor time," and be on hand for other organized events. Working with such a schedule may impede the flexibility of your workday, so consider this factor before applying. The benefit to participating in these meetings and other events is that you can gain valuable information and motivational help. For instance, one organized event at Coldwell Banker is described by a sales agent from Palm Harbor, Florida:

> Our office schedules a friendly competition on weekend or weekday evenings. The sales agents all come to the office; we order a few pizzas and socialize briefly, then make several "cold calls" to try and set up appointments for new listings. Whoever gets a listing that evening from those calls wins the contest. It's a good motivational tool and it makes cold calling a little easier since we all do it together.

Another benefit to working for a national franchise is that the cost of doing business is decreased. Many of your office supplies will either be supplied free of charge, or at greatly reduced rates. The parent company can buy in bulk, thereby greatly reducing the price on popular items such as business cards, magnets, signs, and real estate giveaways.

The Big Five

Below are listed the five largest real estate franchises in the country. Together, they employ over 275,000 sales agents. Three of the five largest companies, Century 21, Coldwell Banker, and ERA, are subsidiaries of the Cendant Corporation.

Century 21 (www.century21.com) bills itself as the world's largest residential sales organization. It has over 6,300 independently owned and operated broker offices in over 28 countries.

Coldwell Banker (www.coldwellbanker.com) has 3,000 offices in North America, the Caribbean, Singapore, and Central America.

ERA (www.era.com) is made up of 2,600 brokerages across the United States and in 17 other countries.

RE/MAX (www.remax.com) is the only real estate franchise still owned and operated by its founders. It has 3,700 offices in 35 countries.

Prudential Real Estate (www.prudential.com/realestate/) is owned by the insurance company of the same name, and employs over 40,000 sales associates in 1,500 offices across the country and in Canada.

Large Independent Firms

Independent firms may have many branch offices in one state, region, or city. They are not affiliated with a national franchise, but rather are owned by an independent party. You may find that these firms are similar to national franchises in their organized structure and advanced training programs. However, a major difference is that each real estate office that is owned by a large independent firm is most likely headed by an office manager/broker who is not the owner. By comparison, franchised offices are usually managed by the owner/broker of that office. Therefore, with large independent firms, you face a greater likelihood of an office manager relocating to run a different office or to open his or her own office.

One advantage of working for such a firm is that they may offer more management opportunities. If you think you'd like to advance in your own career to an office manager position, look at the large independent firms near you. Another advantage is that you can get a lot of the perks of a national franchise, without having to pay the franchise royalty out of your commissions, such as the benefit of a name that has built up a significant amount of local recognition in your community. For independent companies that have several branch offices, the name recognition factor can prove crucial in a local region.

Small Independent Firms

Small independent firms have one or two branch offices. Most often, they are run by an owner/broker and employ a handful of sales agents. Other independent firms may have only one office, but it is larger, with 30–40 sales agents. Some independent firms specialize in a particular type of real estate, such as waterfront homes, commercial real estate, or upscale condominiums or other special types of property. They may have become experts in their area of specialization and have built up a name for themselves in their community. These can be good firms to work for if you want to learn their area of specialization or if you want to get into their niche market in a local area.

You may have more flexibility in a small independent firm since it probably won't require as many formal sales meetings or other training sessions for its agents. Often, training will be informal and may consist of a conversation with a broker over a cup of coffee instead of a formal classroom atmosphere. This type of office can be a good bet for someone who wants to work part time or who needs extensive flexibility in his or her hours and in the demands placed on him or her by the office. Indeed, independent firms are increasingly encouraging part-time sales agents, while the franchise offices are discouraging or forcing them out.

Regardless of the type and size of the company you feel would be a good match for your personality and career goals, you need to know how to evaluate each individual office that you visit to see if you'd like to join that firm.

HOW TO EVALUATE A REAL ESTATE OFFICE

Your future success depends not only on your professional abilities, but also on the company that you work for. In other words, where you work may be almost as important as how you work. Keeping this in mind, there are a number of things to consider as you investigate the real estate companies you regard as possible places of employment. Some may seem obvious, while others may not have occurred to you before. All of them add up to a complete picture of the company you may work for, and it is this picture that you should size up before making a decision as to where to work.

Location

Where is the company located? If you aren't willing to add a long commute into your daily schedule, begin by looking at real estate offices located near where you live. Evaluate each office based on the amount of public contact it encourages. Is the location in a busy place? Does it have a large sign that is easily seen by people driving by? Are there other stores and offices nearby that may encourage foot traffic to the office? Does the building look attractive, and is it easily spotted from the street? These are all pluses.

Inside the Office

As you walk up the sidewalk to the door, how does the landscaping look? Is there any? Can you see through the windows? Is there good lighting on the sidewalk and in the parking lot for evening appointments? As you open the door and walk inside the building, what sight greets you? Is there a waiting room, and if so, does it look comfortable? Try to view the area immediately inside the doorway as a prospective client would see it. Is there a friendly atmosphere? Does the office project a professional image, or is it messy? You want to find an office that appeals to prospective clients and customers as well as to yourself. You'll eventually be meeting and greeting your own customers in the waiting area, so you want to make sure it meets your standards.

Take a look at how many desks there are and how they are organized. Will you have any privacy? Are there shared offices or conference rooms that you can use when customers want to speak to you privately? Some people may not feel comfortable discussing their credit histories or income levels with you in the middle of a large room surrounded by hordes of other agents and customers.

What about Advertising?

This could well be the single most important factor in your decision-making. Effective advertising leads to name recognition, making a company's image common to the general population. If you work for a company that has such recognition, your job is made easier, because people will associate you with the quality and success of your company before you even say a word. Today, marketing takes many forms beyond the traditional print, radio, and television ads. Companies sponsor sporting events, music concerts, and stadiums, for example.

When examining your prospective employer's marketing campaign(s) you should look at the following factors. First, collect the printed advertising from several different real estate companies to see how they compare. How is the overall quality of each ad? What type of paper is it printed on—glossy high quality color paper or black-and-white newsprint? How are the ads worded? Do they sound high-pressured in their approach? Do the ads have a professional appearance?

Note any other types of advertising that the real estate company does, such as billboards, radio and television advertisements, or a telephone hotline. Investigate each of these areas to see how much of a presence each real estate company has. Advertising can directly impact your business if it is done well, by providing you with leads to both buyers and sellers.

If you are seeking a company that specializes in commercial real estate or appraisal, you may not find any printed advertisements aimed at the general public. Instead, you may need to ask around to find out where their advertising appears. They may choose to market themselves in specific industry publications and marketing brochures, which are sent to related businesses.

Check Out Their Website

Search the Internet to see if each company has a website. It, too, should be evaluated using many of the criteria listed above. Most real estate company websites include information both for prospective clients as well as prospective salespeople. The national franchises have sites that include property listings, mortgage information, neighborhood searches, and job listings (see page 93 for their addresses). You can find other companies' sites by using a search engine, using the name of the company as the search term(s). Good sites for searching include:

www.hotbot.lycos.com
www.excite.com
www.altavista.com
www.askjeeves.com
www.fastsearch.com

JUST THE FACTS

Coldwell Banker reports that its website gets over 8 million hits and generates over 3,000 leads each month. When a potential client asks for information, he or she is directed to a local office, which can translate into a listing, a sale, or both, for that office.

JOB SEARCHING ON THE INTERNET

One of the fastest growing resources for job searching is the Internet. Many individual companies maintain websites that describe their company, its purpose, and job openings. Other sites are useful for job searching in general, providing guidance in topics such as resume and cover letter writing. Some sites specialize in networking or "headhunting;" you post your resume and other information about yourself, and hiring companies can search for and view your information when looking for new employees. Following are some useful online resources you should take advantage of during your job search.

Real Estate Websites

www.real-jobs.com
> This site, which requires a $10.00 fee for posting resumes (free if you're a full-time student), contains commercial real estate jobs and resume profiles, experience and skill descriptions, and salary requirements by area.

www.realbank.com
> This real estate site has a resume bank for real estate professionals to find jobs and post resumes and profiles; it includes a searchable employment opportunities section.

www.cob.ohio-state.edu/~fin/jobs/realest.htm
> Ohio State University's Fisher College of Business/Real Estate maintains this site that contains information on skill requirements in real estate, job descriptions, print and Internet resources, salaries, facts, and trends.

www.realestatejobstore.com
> After submitting your resume, sign up here for a "job search agent," which e-mails you the job postings that match your search requirements. You can also find employer profiles and help with your resume here.

www.inrealty.com/rejob.html
> You will find a number of links here to sites providing employment listings, as well as direct links to companies with available positions.

nyu.edu/library/rei

The Jack Brause Library at New York University's Real Estate Institute maintains this site that has discussion groups, web links, e-journals, online newspapers, and searchable databases of information regarding real estate.

www.jobsite.com

This site specializes in real estate, and includes a salary survey, company profiles, job listings, and a resume posting service.

Career-Related Websites

www.jobsfed.com

The best site for government jobs; it lists over 10,000.

www.headhunter.net/JobSeeker/Index.htm

Over 250,000 jobs are listed on this site; you can save job search results, and post your resume as well.

www.monster.com

A large number of job openings are posted here; assistance such as resume editing is also offered.

www.jobbankusa.com

A major source of job postings and career information.

www.careerbuilder.com

Find advice on cover letters, resumes, interviewing, and negotiating job offers here. You can post your resume, or submit it to a hiring company online, as well as search over 75 sites for job listings.

IN THE NEWS

Mortgage and real estate companies are beginning to experiment with "paperless" or electronic closings, in which real estate may be financed, bought, and sold without the usual mountain of documents that must be signed by all parties. These closings are possible because of the federal E-SIGN legislation signed into law by President Clinton on June 30, 2000. Passage of the federal legislation allows a nationwide adoption of electronic signatures and documents as legally binding for various types of business transactions, including home mortgages.

NETWORKING

Networking—the art of making contact with others to obtain information or to get help meeting a specific goal, is a major job search tactic used by people in all industries. However, it is especially important in real estate because the field focuses so much on interacting with people. Examples of real estate job search networking include asking sales agents if they like the company they work for, and asking friends and relatives if they know of a great broker in your area who would be an excellent mentor. Networking with real estate professionals can give you inside information on local trends. You can also find out about what other companies are doing and which brokers are hiring. Additionally, you may get the scoop on which brokers hold the greatest market share in the area of specialization that you want to pursue. Once you land a job, you will network with nearly everyone you meet, in order to build up a client base, getting new property listings or finding qualified buyers (Chapter 5 explains this type of networking in greater detail).

The subject of networking is intimidating to some, who picture it as insincere small talk or handshaking. However, when it is done properly, it is completely sincere, and can benefit both parties involved. The key to successful networking is to break down the process into easy-to-follow steps. We will explore these steps below, showing each one's direct application to a real estate job search.

Step One: Identify Small Goals

Of course your ultimate goal, not only for networking, but for the entire job search process, is to find a great job. However, you shouldn't approach day-to-day networking as a means to that larger goal. Instead, as your first step, identify smaller goals that can be met quickly. For instance, you have narrowed down your search to three real estate offices in your area. Now, you want to get "inside" information about these offices in order to decide which one you want to apply for a job with, or, you may simply be seeking advice from those already working in the field. Once your goals are identified, you can best determine how to meet them.

Step Two: Be Informed

If your goal is to seek advice about commercial real estate in your area, get as much information on your own as you can. Research the companies that deal in this type of real estate; you should be able to find out about them on the Internet. Also understand the field in general. You want to sound like you have done your homework when you begin to make contacts.

This is also the step in which you begin to make a list of potential contacts that may help you meet your goal(s). Print ads in newspapers and local magazines may feature top sales agents, or list all of the agents working in a particular office. The students and teachers you meet through real estate education are also good candidates for this list.

Step Three: Make a Connection

Using the list of potential contacts you developed in step two, build a network of sales agents who work at the offices you are interested in joining. Call them, or visit their offices. (If you were unable to come up with a list of specific people, call or visit the offices, asking to talk to at least one of the real estate agents in each.) Although busy, most agents will take a few minutes to speak with a prospective newcomer. They were new to the business once themselves, so if you are careful not to take up too much of their time, they will probably be glad to give you some information. Begin by introducing yourself, showing that you are informed (Step 2) and interested in what they have to say. Then, ask if they are willing to help you.

Step Four: Ask for What You Want

If your contact indicates that he or she is willing to help you, be honest and direct about what you want. If your goal is to find out inside information about the office in which a contact works, tell her that you are thinking of applying to work there. Then, ask questions such as:

- ▶ "How do you like the office?"
- ▶ "What are the benefits of working here?"
- ▶ "What is the office atmosphere like?"
- ▶ "Where else have you worked, and how does this office compare?"

Step Five: Expand Your Network

We spoke in Step 4 about being direct with your contacts. This is also true when seeking to expand your network. One of the most valuable pieces of information you can get from a contact is another contact. After you've gotten the information you need to meet your Step 1 goal(s), simply ask if he or she would mind sharing with you the name of another person who might also be able to help you.

Step Six: Organize Yourself

You have probably already written down your goals, and made lists of contacts. Once you've spoken with some of them, organization becomes even more important. You will need to keep track of your contacts, as well as the information you receive. You may need to connect with this person again in the future, and want to be able to easily access your information. There are software packages that can help you to keep track of your networking contacts or you can simply use a notebook and organize yourself. For each contact, note:

- ▶ Name
- ▶ Address
- ▶ E-mail address
- ▶ Phone number (work, pager, cellular phone, residence)
- ▶ Fax number
- ▶ Company name
- ▶ Job title
- ▶ First meeting—where, when, the topics you discussed
- ▶ Last contact—when, why, and how

Step Seven: Maintain Your Contacts

It is important to maintain your contacts once you have established them. Try to reach people again within a couple of weeks of meeting them. You can send a note of thanks, ask a question, or send a piece of information related to your conversation with them. This contact cements your meeting in their minds, so they will remember you more readily when you call them again in the future. If you haven't communicated with your contacts for a few months, you might send them a note or e-mail about an article you read, or relevant new technology or law to keep your name fresh in their minds.

PROFESSIONAL ORGANIZATIONS: THE NATIONAL ASSOCIATION OF REALTORS®

Another way to network is to join a group of real estate professionals. Not only can you get information to help you with your job search, but your affiliation with such a group can also help you throughout your career in a number of ways. The National Association of REALTORS® (NAR) is the nation's largest organization of real estate professionals (as well as the largest trade and professional association of any kind). It was founded in 1908, and currently has almost 750,000 members. Members are known as REAL-TORS®, and include brokers, salespeople, property managers, appraisers, counselors, and others involved in the real estate industry. They first join one of 1,700 local associations/boards, and membership is then extended to the state and national associations. Members are pledged to a strict Code of Ethics and Standards of Practice (to read it, log onto www.realtor.com).

The NAR is active politically, both by financing lobbyists who work to protect its members' interests, and by encouraging the involvement of its members in the campaigns of candidates backed by the NAR. Members have access to industry information and each other through a website (www.one-realtorplace.com), a magazine, meetings, and conventions. They can network, find news about changing legislation that may affect their business, and do research at an online real estate library. Roberta Dinerstein, an agent in Boca Raton, Florida, notes that

> The NAR does good work for REALTORS®, especially by lobbying for our causes nationwide. This does seep down to the state and local levels. For so many years, REALTORS® had a public relations problem, and I believe that has really improved.

As mentioned in Chapter 2, the NAR offers professional designations that are awarded after successful completion of required coursework. They also offer membership in special sub-groups that provide their members with the support and information they need in their careers. These groups include Counselors of Real Estate, Commercial Investment Real Estate Institute, Institute of Real Estate Management, REALTORS® Land Institute, REALTORS® National Marketing Institute®, Real Estate Brokerage Managers Council, Residential Sales Council, Real Estate Buyers Agent Council, Society of Industrial and Office REALTORS®, Women's Council of REALTORS®, Appraisal Section, and International Section.

Once you've networked for information, and completed your job search, your membership in the National Association of REALTORS® can continue to be of great use. The NAR maintains www.realtor.com, the largest online source of real estate listings. As a member, you will be listed on the site, so that prospective clients may find you. All of your listings and open houses can also be uploaded for viewing by anyone around the world. The NAR's website also allows you to conduct real-time conversations with those who view your listings. By using these resources, you can potentially see a great increase in your business.

WRITING YOUR RESUME

A resume gives prospective employers a history of your skills, education, and work experience. It may either be their first contact with you (if you've sent it to them before making any other contact), or a written reminder of your qualifications (after you've met and gone through an interview). While there are many different formats for resumes, all resumes should contain the following information:

► name, address, telephone number, e-mail address if applicable
► employment objective—the type of work or specific job you're looking for
► work experience—job title, name and address of employer, dates of employment (you may want to include part time and volunteer positions)
► description of duties you performed on your previous job(s)
► education, including school name(s) and address(es), dates of attendance, highest grade completed, or type of certification, diploma, or degree awarded
► special skills, knowledge of computer programs, proficiency in foreign languages, and honors or awards
► membership in professional organizations or associations (when applicable)
► professional qualifications or certifications

How to Organize Your Resume

The two most common types of resumes are:

► the chronological format
► the functional (or skills) format

In the chronological format, you list the dates of your past employment in chronological order. This is a good format for people who have continuous work experience with little or no gaps in employment. The functional resume is used when there is not a stable work history; instead of emphasizing each prior position held, the functional resume highlights specific skills and achievements. Resume experts agree that the functional resume should only be used when absolutely necessary, as it may be viewed as a "red flag" to a prospective employer, alerting him to the fact that you may have been at fault somehow in creating an unstable employment history.

However, if you must write a functional resume, there are ways in which to make it stand out. The sample resumes beginning on page 110 will give you some ideas about how best to put yourself on paper for potential employers. You may also want to log on to some of the employment sites listed beginning on page 98, many of which offer advice on resume writing. Other examples can be found in publications available through your public library or local bookstore (see Appendix A for a list of books about writing resumes).

The length and variety of your work experience is your best guide to your resume's length, but one page is generally preferred for a standard resume, and never longer than two. When you've finished writing your resume, ask someone you trust to read it and suggest ways to improve it.

Resume Tips and Techniques

Here are a few additional suggestions for preparing your resume:

▶ Use standard-letter-size ivory, cream, or neutral colored paper. Smaller size resumes may get thrown out or lost and larger sized ones will get crumpled edges.

▶ Include your name, address, and phone number on every page (if longer than one page).

▶ Emphasize your name by either making it larger than anything else on the page, or by making it bold or italic, or some combination thereof.

▶ Use a font that is easy to read, such as 12-point Times New Roman.

▶ Do not use more than three fonts in your resume.

▶ Prepare several different resumes, emphasizing skills the various companies or organizations you're applying to are looking for.

▶ Be positive and confident in your resume, but don't lie or embellish heavily.

▶ Proofread your final draft very carefully. Read it forward and backward. Have your friends with good proofreading skills read it. Even if you have a grammar and spell checker on your computer, you still need to review it. For instance, a spell checker would not catch any of the errors in the following sentence: Their are two many weighs too make errors that an computer does nut recognize.

▶ Use bullet points instead of long sentences.

▶ Include key words that are important in your industry.

▶ Don't include personal information on your resume such as your birthdate, race, marital status, religion, or height.

▶ Do not crowd your resume—shorten the margins if you need more space.

▶ Use action words, such as managed, conducted, developed, or produced.

▶ Be consistent when using boldface, capitalization, underlining, and italics. If one company name is underlined, make sure all are underlined. Check titles and dates too.

▶ Keep your resume updated. Don't write "9/97 to Present," if you ended your job two months ago. Such errors could be perceived as misrepresentation.

▶ Do not cross out anything or handwrite any comments on your resume.

▶ Understand and remember everything written on your resume. Be able to back up all statements with specific examples.

What Is a Computer Scanned Resume?

Many large companies today are using optical character recognition (OCR) scanning systems to store the resumes they receive from job applicants in a computer database. Then, when they want to fill a position, they type in keywords to search the database for the most relevant resumes. While you probably won't run into this method of recruiting in a small, local, independent real estate office, you will be likely to find such a system in place in large property management firms or corporate headquarters of the largest real estate franchises. If you believe that the company for which you want to work employs this technology, prepare your resume by following these basic guidelines:

▶ Left-justify the entire document (don't use tabs or indents).

▶ Use a font such as Ariel, in which each letter is completely separate (fonts such as Times Roman have little "feet" on most letters that may make those letters appear joined together, and therefore unreadable by the scanner).

▶ Don't condense your type.

▶ Use normal line spacing—don't cram the lines together to get more information on the resume.

▶ Use bold and capital letters for emphasis (not underlining or italics).

▶ Avoid light type and paper that is too dark.

▶ Don't include any horizontal lines, parentheses, or brackets.

▶ Avoid italics, script, underlining, columns, newsletter layout, and graphics.

▶ Use only simple bullet points, such as black circles.

▶ Use more than one page if necessary.

▶ Print in crisp black ink on a laser printer—do not send a fax or a photocopy.

▶ Use key words that you think a recruiter might search for.

▶ Use spaces between dashes and ampersands between the text (1999–2000; A & M Inc.).

▶ Don't fold your resume—send it in a large envelope.

A further note on keywords: these are the words an employer will search for in her database of resumes. Before adapting your resume to be scannable, think as if you were the recruiter. What skills, education, and work experience would you look for in a new employee? Make a list of the keywords that might be searched for, such as: "management," "manager," "_____ years experience," "MS Word," "training program," "Excel." Be aware that keywords are generally nouns. When you create a scannable resume try to use nouns to highlight your experience and skills rather than verbs. For example, rather than using an "action verb" such as "managed" use the noun "manager" instead. The more potential keywords you include on your resume, the greater chance you'll have of getting it read.

ASCII Resumes

If you are asked to e-mail your resume, you may need to send it as a plain text document, which will be readable regardless of the word processing software used by the hiring company. To create an ASCII resume, you will need to remove all formatting codes, such as special fonts, boldface, italics, or underlined text, graphics, etc. Use the guidelines given on page 107 to help you, keeping in mind that the resume you e-mail may end up scanned, too. Even if you send a scannable or ASCII resume, take regularly formatted resumes with you to your interviews. Human readers will appreciate the formatting you put into it.

Many employers can also accept a formatted document that is sent as an attachment. Sending your resume as an attachment to an e-mailed cover letter is a preferable method because you can preserve the professional appearance of your formatted document. It is best if you can check with the employer to see which method of electronic submission he or she prefers.

References

Employers interested in hiring you may want to speak to people who can accurately describe your work experience and personal qualities—people known in job search terms as references. How do you come up with references? The first step is to make a list of people (other than relatives) who know you well and who would recommend you to an employer. Ask those on your list for permission to use them as references. Then, narrow down your list to the two or three people you feel would best represent you to a potential employer.

It is standard practice to state at the bottom of the resume that you have references available upon request. However some career experts consider this line on a resume unnecessary because it should be understood that any applicant should be prepared to provide references. Sometimes space will dictate your decision whether to include this line, otherwise it is a personal choice. If you are responding to an advertisement, read it carefully to see if you are asked to send your list of references. List them on a sheet of paper separate from your resume, but remember to include your name, address, and phone number on the top of the list. For each reference, provide the following information:

- ▶ name
- ▶ address
- ▶ telephone number
- ▶ job title

You may not need to provide a separate list of references, but it's handy to carry one along on job interviews. If you are asked to complete an application, you can easily fill in the information about each reference. Once you have perfected your resume, you'll need to write a well-crafted cover letter.

Sample Chronological Resume

JACQUELINE DAWSON

524 Hercules Avenue

Santa Barbara, CA 91123

816-459-9836

OBJECTIVE: Real Estate Sales Agent

EXPERIENCE

1999–Present   Aimes Mortgage Company

296 Rosemary Court

Santa Barbara, CA 91125

Administrative assistant to owner

- Ordered, organized, and analyzed credit reports
- Pre-qualified buyers for specific loan programs
- Maintained files and records, did light bookkeeping
- Assisted manager with marketing duties
- Composed and typed correspondence

1998–1999   Glass Block Designs

126 Colorado Boulevard

Pasadena, CA 91054

Sales Clerk

- Worked part time while in high school
- Learned basic selling techniques
- Operated cashier machine

EDUCATION

Certificate in Real Estate Principles and Practices (29 credit hours)

from El Camino College, Torrance, CA. 2000

Diploma. Valley High School. Pasadena, CA, 1998

QUALIFICATIONS AND SKILLS

Familiar with Windows 3.1 and Windows 95

Excellent time-management and organizational skills

Excellent written and verbal communications skills

Sample Functional Resume

HABIB HUSNI

1916 York Drive

Jersey City, NJ 52245

718-784-2358

OBJECTIVE:	Residential Real Estate Broker
QUALIFICATIONS	• Three years of experience as residential sales agent • State Licensed as Residential Real Estate Sales Agent • Extensive knowledge of real estate trends, market, and laws
PROFESSIONAL EXPERIENCE	• Experienced in using real estate computer software • Wrote manual for training new sales agents • Experienced in filling in for office manager • Skilled at conducting weekly agent meetings • Ordered office supplies and worked accounts payable for brokerage
EMPLOYMENT HISTORY	Real Estate Sales Agent, Brynmeiser Associates, Inc., 1998–Present Real Estate Sales Agent, Finger Lakes Realty Corp., 1997–1998
EDUCATION	B.A. in Business Administration with a concentration in Real Estate from Cornell University in Ithaca, New York, 1998 65 hours of continuing education credits from the Career Pro Real Estate School, Hoboken, New Jersey National Association of REALTORS® GRI Designation

Sample Scannable Resume

CHRIS NYUGEN
1450 Ocean View Court
San Diego, CA 94555
415-555-9876

Objective	Property Manager
Keywords	General Manager, Lease Negotiation, Income and Expense Reports, Customer Service, Communicator, Bachelor of Arts, Commercial Real Estate, Investment Properties

Skills

- successful in lease negotiations
- manage sub-contractors
- research land use
- proficient in Microsoft Word for Windows, Excel, Lotus 1-2-3
- experienced in customer relations and service—friendly, professional, personable
- excellent written and verbal communication skills
- self-motivated, independent worker

Professional Highlights

Macy Property Management, Inc.
Assistant Property Manager, 1997–present
San Diego, CA
Duties:

- collect and deposit rental payments for 52 units
- handle lease negotiations
- complete accounts receivable and payable reports
- secure and manage sub-contractors
- respond to tenant complaints

Grove Apartment Village
San Diego, CA
On-Site Residence Manager, 1988–1993
Duties:

- collect and deposit rents for 16 units
- conduct move-out inspections of properties
- perform routine maintenance for tenants
- obtain sub-contractors for major repairs
- maintain income and expense log

Education

Bachelor of Business Administration. Major: Real Estate
University of Georgia, 1997

WRITING COVER LETTERS

A cover letter is a way to introduce and sell yourself to prospective employers. It should be brief and capture the employer's attention, letting him or her know what you can do for them. The cover letter should not be used to repeat what is in your resume. Follow a business letter format, and include the following information:

- ▶ The name and address of the specific person to whom the letter is addressed
- ▶ The title of the job for which you are applying
- ▶ The reason for your interest in the company or position
- ▶ Your main qualifications for the position (in brief)
- ▶ A request for an interview
- ▶ Your phone number and address

Your first paragraph should serve as an introduction that grabs the hiring manager's attention. Indicate why you are sending your resume; speak of your interest in the company and the specific position for which you are applying. If you are responding to an advertisement in the newspaper, you can copy the job title directly out of the advertisement; the hiring manager probably wrote the ad and is very familiar with the terminology. Many human resources departments track the success of their ads, so include the source where you saw the position advertised.

Take the time to do some investigating, so you can address your cover letter to someone in particular. Call the company and ask for the hiring manager's name or the Human Resource representative's name. If it is the company's policy not to give out names, at least get the person's formal title and use that in place of the person's name. If there is any connection between you and that person or her company, state it clearly in the first paragraph. Mention that you work in the same field, have common interests, or that you have knowledge of the company.

In the body of your cover letter, summarize your qualifications effectively. You don't have room to list the details of all the jobs you have held, so try to come up with a powerful summary such as, "I have three years experience in real estate residential sales and two years experience in industrial sales." In this way, you are drawing attention to the most important part of your resume, while showing your prospective employer how he can benefit from hiring you. Think about what the company wants from the person who will get the position, and be sure to explain how you can give it.

End your cover letter with a plan for action. Tell the hiring manager how to reach you (phone number, e-mail address), but also indicate that you will call him or her if you haven't heard back in a few days. Say that you would like to schedule an interview at his or her earliest convenience. Be polite, but also show some assertiveness. Once you have sent out your resume and cover letter, follow up as you indicated you would, and schedule an interview.

Sample Cover Letter

76 Round Street, Apt. 10

Kansas City, MO 64112

June 8, 2001

Ms. Valerie Williams

Office Manager

ABC Realty

1916 Main Street, Suite 304

Kansas City, MO 64110

Dear Ms. Williams:

I am applying for the position of residential sales agent listed in *The Kansas City Star* on June 7, 2001. I am familiar with your company, and know that it provides excellent agent training and support for motivated, qualified people such as myself.

As you can see from my enclosed resume, I have worked in sales for two years. During that time, I completed the education requirement for my state real estate agent's license. I am a Kansas City native, and know first-hand the many selling points of living in our city. That knowledge, combined with my sales experience and real estate education, have prepared me for a career in residential real estate sales, and makes me an excellent candidate for this position.

I look forward to hearing from you, and may be reached by phone at (816) 762-1234 or by e-mail at milinkovich@smartsite.com. Or, I will contact you within the next week, to arrange an interview at your convenience. Thank you in advance for your time and consideration.

Sincerely,

Joshua Milinkovich

Enclosure

SUCCEEDING IN AN INTERVIEW

After you've sent out resumes and cover letters to the real estate company(s) for which you'd like to work, the next hurdle is gaining an interview with the office manager or broker who does the hiring for that office. If you haven't heard from him or her within a week after sending your resume, call to arrange a time for an interview. If she tells you the position is filled and there aren't others open (this will be rare), ask if you can come in for an information interview. From such an interview, you can gain more information about the company, make a good impression, and find out when to re-apply.

Before the Interview

Prepare carefully for each interview—learn as much as you can about the company ahead of time. You will want to sound knowledgeable and confident, and doing your homework will help with both. Another way to gain confidence is by practicing. Using the list of questions below, hold a mock interview with a friend or family member to brush up on your presentation and communication skills. The following table contains some of the most common interview questions and tips on how to answer them.

Question	Answer Tip`
Tell me about yourself.	You should not provide any personal information in your answer (such as marital status, religion, or hobbies that do not relate to real estate sales). Focus on information about your training, qualifications, and work experience. Practice answering this question before you go on an interview; it can be disarming if you're not ready for it.
What are your strengths and weaknesses?	Be honest. They want to know because they are evaluating not only your skills and

education but how well you will fit in to the work environment. If you aren't honest, it will show up eventually. Emphasize your strengths more than your weaknesses and mention only weaknesses that won't break the company.

What do you know about our company?	This is the opportunity to impress the hiring manager by showing that you had the initiative and drive to research the company before you interviewed. Make sure you have something positive to say.
Do you have plans for continuing education?	Most states require that you complete continuing education courses to renew your sales license, so be aware of what those requirements are before you go on an interview. Express enthusiasm for learning more about your chosen profession.
Why did you leave your last job?	No matter how bad the circumstances may have been, always frame your reason in a positive light. You might want to say something like "I wanted more responsibility" or "I wanted more growth opportunities." Don't ever say it was because you hated your boss!

What to Do During the Interview

Greet your interviewer with a firm handshake and an enthusiastic smile. Focus on speaking confidently throughout the interview and answer questions in complete sentences. Aim to keep your answers around two to three minutes each. Try to appear relaxed during your interview—the best ways to do this are to get enough sleep the night before, be prepared when you go in with knowledge about the company, and know the questions you want to ask of your interviewer. Also, make sure to project a professional appearance by dressing neatly and conservatively. Here are a few more tips on how to succeed in an interview:

▶ Arrive early or exactly on time—before the day of the interview, learn where the company is located, and determine how much time you'll need to get to the office.

▶ Know the name of your interviewer and shake hands when you meet.

▶ During the interview, make eye contact, speak clearly, and maintain good posture.

▶ Use standard formal English and avoid slang.

▶ If you're asked about a skill you don't possess, admit it, but say you're willing to learn.

▶ Ask questions about the position and the organization—show enthusiasm and genuine interest.

▶ Thank the interviewer at the completion of the interview.

You need to not only answer questions in an interview clearly and concisely, but you also need to ask questions. Asking the right questions can help to determine if you really want to work for this particular company or organization, while also letting your interviewer know that you are interested and prepared.

Asking Questions

The interviewer will most likely ask you if you have any questions at some point during the interview. If she doesn't, you'll need to bring it up yourself. You can simply say something like, "I also have a few questions for you to help me get a better sense of the position" and then begin asking. Have a list of questions ready in advance. There are many things that you need to know about the company and the hiring manager to determine if the company is a good fit for you. It's not just a one-way street on which they evaluate you— you can also evaluate them. If you don't ask any questions, the hiring manager may think that you aren't interested enough in the position.

Below are questions for prospective real estate sales agents to ask each broker or office manager they interview with:

1. How much market share does your company hold? What are your prospects for growth? While you may not get specific percentages in the answers to these types of questions, you should be supplied with at least a general sense of how the company stacks up against its competitors.

2. What type of management style do you have? If you desire a hands-on manager who will guide you through every step of the way, you'd better listen carefully to this answer. An answer such as "we have a really hands-off management style here" may indicate that you will get minimal guidance after you are hired. On the other hand, perhaps you thrive on independence and prefer this style. In this case, "hands-off" is the answer you are looking for.

3. How many sales agents and how many departments do you have? Large firms generally offer a greater variety of training programs and career options. Employers who have 20 or more agents may also have better office facilities and equipment due to a larger operating budget. If you're thinking about getting into commercial or industrial real estate, you may want to start out at a company that has these departments. However, jobs in small companies may offer more variety and a closer working relationship with your broker.

4. What type of training do you offer? If you plan to obtain your pre-license training through the company that hires you, find out how long the basic training program lasts, if it prepares you to pass your state's licensing exam, if it is recognized by your state as a licensed education provider, and if it includes training on the company's software programs. Even if you have already completed your initial training and licensing, you should ask about the continuing training that the company offers.

5. How do you handle the company's marketing needs? You'll want to pick a company that has a strong marketing strategy that pays off in a successful image and significant public recognition.

6. What are the key qualities that you seek in new salespeople? The answer to this question can help you package yourself later in the interview. At the very least, you'll know what qualities to work on if you get hired.

7. Do you have listing or sales quotas? While quotas may work to motivate some salespeople, you don't want to have too much pressure on you the first year. Find out the penalty for not meeting quotas, if any, and consider it carefully. Not all companies have quotas.

8. What are the average start-up costs for new sales agents? Find out if the company offers any discounts or free items to new agents: business cards, signs, magnets, office supplies.

9. Do you provide errors and omissions insurance? You'll want to find out if the agents pay for it or if the fee is split with the broker.

10. What is the ratio of commission splits you offer to new agents? Can I achieve a more favorable commission split in the future? The industry standard is to give new sales agents 50/50 commission split with the sponsoring broker. However, if you bring in a certain amount of money, you should be able to negotiate a higher split. Some companies have an organized system, such as if you bring in $30,000 worth of commissions in a year, then you get to keep 60% of the commission, instead of 50%, and so on up to a maximum level.

Follow-up After the Interview

Send a note to the interviewer, thanking him for the opportunity to speak with him. It is best to send your thank-you note immediately after your interview. Mention the time and date of the original interview and any important points discussed. Discuss any qualifications that you may have omitted in the interview, and reiterate your interest in the job.

Don't be discouraged if a definite offer was not made at the interview. The interviewer will usually communicate with his office staff or interview other applicants before making an offer. Generally, a decision is reached within a few weeks. If you do not hear from an employer within the amount of time suggested during the interview, follow up with a telephone call. Show your commitment to their timetable by waiting the correct number of days or weeks, and by not calling repeatedly.

THE INFORMATIONAL INTERVIEW

If a company you're interested in does not have any room to take on a new salesperson when you are conducting your job search, you may want to conduct an informational interview either with the broker/office manager or another salesperson. These interviews are a good way to get more information about the industry in general, as well as the particular company. Make maximum use of the time a person is willing to spend with you by being prepared to ask pertinent questions concisely. Below is a list of good questions to ask during an informational interview:

▶ What is your typical workday like?

▶ What things do you find most rewarding about your work?

▶ What are the toughest problems you encounter in your job?

▶ Can you give me a general description of the work you do?

▶ What are the frustrations in your work?

▶ If you could change your job in some way, what would that change be?

▶ What educational degrees, licenses, or other credentials are required for entry and advancement in your kind of work? Are there any in particular that are preferred or helpful?

▶ What are the trade/professional groups to which you belong, and which do you find most beneficial in your work? Do any of them assist people who are interested in entry-level positions in your field?

▶ What abilities, interests, values, and personality characteristics are important for effectiveness and satisfaction in your field?

▶ How do people usually learn about job openings in your field?

▶ What types of employers, other than your own, hire people to perform the type of work you do? Do you know of any which offer entry-level training programs or opportunities?

▶ If you were hiring someone for an entry-level position in your field, what would be the critical factors influencing your choice of one candidate over another?

▶ Is there anything else you think I would benefit from knowing about this field?

Conducting informational interviews will not only make you more knowledgeable about your prospective position, but it will also give you interview experience, which may lessen the anxiety in an actual job interview. An informational interview is also an excellent opportunity for you to learn more about how different companies work, and to gain a contact that might help you get a job in the future.

MONEY ISSUES

As we've discussed in this chapter, interviews for a position as a real estate agent differ from most other job interviews in that salary is not an issue. When the issue of money arises, it is regarding the size of commissions (how much the agent and office each get to keep), and who pays for expenses such as Errors and Omissions Insurance, continuing education credits, and tools of the trade (cell phone, laptop, etc.). This is because agents are basically self-employed, earning a percentage of each sale in which they represent a client. Therefore, before landing a job, you should have a financial plan for dealing with the likely scenario of many months without an income.

Before you make your first sale, you will need to develop a list of clients, or potential clients. If you're working for a large company, you may be provided with leads. Whether buying or selling, it can take months before your clients are ready to close a deal, meaning months in which your hard work does not pay off financially. Even when your first closing takes place, it may be months before your second. If you haven't planned ahead for this scenario, it can mean the end of your career before it has a chance to really start. You will need to think now about how you will pay for living (and work-related) expenses during this start-up time. Have you saved enough to live on for at least six months? Can you rely on family members to help you out during the early days of your career? Do you have a source from which you can borrow money before you begin to see some success?

EVALUATING JOB OFFERS

After all the work you've put into your job search, you're beginning to get job offers. In fact, if you're looking for a job as a real estate salesperson, chances are that you will be offered several jobs. Most likely, the companies that offer you a position will not expect you to accept or reject an offer on the spot. You'll probably have a week or more to make up your mind. Your task is to re-evaluate each company that wants to hire you. Go back to the beginning of this chapter and review the section on evaluating a company. How does each company stack up against the other? Perhaps one will reimburse your tuition, perhaps another one is right next door to your home, perhaps a third one has a great broker with whom you really clicked.

Take a look at all of your options, review your notes from the interviews, and then make a list of the pros and cons for joining each company. Then, look at the list and choose the company with the most powerful pros and the least important cons. When you've made a selection, contact the hiring manager or broker, who will give you information about training, and when to report for work.

The job search process can be complex and time-consuming. But by taking the process one step at a time, armed with the information in this chapter, you can succeed. Once you start your new career, you'll want to consult Chapter 5, to learn how to take your success on the job with you.

THE INSIDE TRACK

Who: Roberta Dinerstein
What: Real Estate Agent-Broker
Where: Arvida Realty Services, Boca Raton, Florida
How Long: Licensed agent for over 20 years

INSIDER'S STORY

After buying my own home over 20 years ago, I decided I wanted to enter the real estate field. A few years earlier, I helped a relative study for his broker exam, so I was familiar with the jargon and felt the excitement of "the deal." Real estate was a good match for me because, at the time I entered it, you could work out of your home much of the time, and I wouldn't have a boss looking over my shoulder. This was important since I had two young children. I also didn't have a college degree, and this is one field in which you can achieve success without one.

I started work in New York, and then moved to Florida about 10 years later. I've found Florida to be much more of a challenge for sales work. First, more territory is covered, so you spend more time in your car. Second, most buyers are from out-of-state, so you may work with them for a longer period of time before a sale takes place. Third, attorneys are not required for closings, so the salesperson writes the contract with the buyer, and this requires much more classroom education to be able to do well. Last, working in real estate in Florida is more expensive; I must pay for long distance phone service, rent (for my desk), Errors and Omissions insurance, and annual membership in the Board of REALTORS®.

INSIDER'S ADVICE

I would recommend that anyone starting out in the field seek out a position as an "on-site" salesperson—working as the sales agent exclusively for a new development. This means your "office" is where new homes are being constructed, and your broker has contracted with the builder or developer to have you sell the homes there. On-site sales-people gain knowledge of construction and building maintenance that they would probably not get anywhere else. You learn about plumbing, electrical work, roofing, painting, and landscaping, to name a few.

You will also get experience dealing with the public (some wonderful people, others difficult) on an intimate level, as they share information about their finances, their families, and their hopes and dreams. Almost daily contact with attorneys for the developer or builder, the buyers, and the sellers, will give you a good working knowledge of the legal aspects of the field. After a year and half of working as an on-site salesperson, during which 72 homes were sold, I went into general sales. I found that having a background in on-site sales was a great help.

CHAPTER five

SUCCEEDING ON THE JOB

THIS CHAPTER shows how you can succeed once you've landed a job in real estate. You'll find out the qualities that are rewarded, how to interact best with superiors and the public, and how to increase your level of success. Advancement opportunities and career options related to real estate are clearly explained.

YOU CAN achieve success in your real estate career in many different ways. Some professionals stay in sales for the duration of their careers, succeeding as their ever-widening network brings them commission after commission. Others choose to become brokers, managing offices or opening their own companies. Another option is to take a career path related to real estate, such as land developer or mortgage broker. Whichever alternative you decide to pursue, use the tips provided in this chapter to help you reach your goals.

SUCCEEDING IN REAL ESTATE SALES

After you land your first job as a real estate sales agent, you'll receive some type of on-the-job training to augment your pre-licensing education. In large offices that are a part of a national franchise, the training will probably be extensive and highly organized. In smaller, independent offices, your training may consist of teaming up with an experienced sales agent or a broker who will demonstrate common real estate practices as he works. In any form, this training is invaluable, as it teaches you the actual practice of the information you have so far just read about.

Once you begin working, you'll need to negotiate yourself and your clients through a mountain of paperwork, much of which is legally binding. Ask questions of experienced sales agents and your broker until you understand the procedures. It is in their best interest to help you get off to a great start, without making costly mistakes. To get an idea of what to expect, read through the listing contract found in Appendix D, which is used by agents in Nebraska. Other states use very similar forms.

We've polled many successful professionals in the business to find out their best advice to those starting out. Below is a list of their tips.

Starting Out Success Tips

- **Get Business Cards Printed, and Give Them Away**. If your office doesn't provide them, check the yellow pages and find a source to have them printed. Consider the option of including your photo on the card. Start handing out your business cards ASAP to get the ball rolling.

- **Get on the Company Computers**. Practice working with all the computer software that is available in your office. You don't want to wait until you have clients sitting in front of you to discover you don't know how to maneuver the software to fit their particular situation.

- **Broadcast Your Availability**. Tell everyone you know that you are now a real estate sales agent. This includes family, friends, acquaintances, associates, and anyone else you can think of. Even if they won't need your services, they may know of someone who will.

■ **Complete Sample Forms**. You will be amazed at how helpful this is when you begin working with buyers and sellers. You can produce the completed sample forms, highlighted with any pertinent notes and use them to help you complete the actual forms needed.

DRAWING FROM YOUR NETWORK

We discussed networking to find a job in Chapter 4. Now, consider the network you developed as a list of business prospects. Some modifications will be needed, such as the exclusion of any real estate professionals, and the inclusion of many people you already know, who may not have been part of your job search effort. They could include:

▶ Friends and relatives
▶ Current or past coworkers or fellow students
▶ Former teachers
▶ People you've met at meetings, parties, or even at the airport
▶ People you meet in the supermarket
▶ The person who cuts your hair
▶ Your children's friends' parents
▶ Other salespeople who approach you to sell something
▶ Secretaries or other professionals at various offices you may visit on personal business
▶ People who work in related industries who could give you referrals

To expand your network base, ask those in your network for the names of other people who may need the services of a real estate salesperson. Continue to "grow" your list of prospective clients in this way, not just as you are starting out, but throughout your career. Get your name out to as many people as possible—most of them will buy and/or sell a house, and know others who will.

DEVELOPING THE QUALITIES THAT COUNT

When you are interviewed for a real estate sales position, your potential employer looks for qualities in your personality and on your resume that show you will be an asset to his or her company. If she feels you have enough of those qualities, she'll offer you a position. It is at this point, after you are hired, that you may need to focus on those areas in which you may be lacking. Working hard to develop the qualities that spell success for a real estate sales agent will not only improve your business, but will also bring in more commissions to your office, gaining the attention of your coworkers and superiors. This will help you later, if you decide you'd like to move into management or brokering.

Some of these qualities are fairly easy to improve upon. They include a solid educational background and good technical skills. To advance in these areas, you can take courses, read books, practice using real estate software, and rely on a mentor's advice and guidance. Other necessary qualities are more personal, and may take more of an effort to upgrade. Take a look at the list below, and see if any of these areas are ones in which you believe you may be lacking. They include:

Self-Motivation

Since your success depends almost entirely upon your own efforts, you need to be highly motivated. Your motivation to succeed will give you the energy you need to place cold calls and drum up new business when things are slow. It is a challenge to stay motivated when you are not getting paid per hour or on a straight salary. You need to remember that your hard work will pay off in commission checks if you persevere and continually motivate yourself.

Public Interaction Skills

Since your work revolves around people—sellers, buyers, tenants, mortgage bankers, lawyers, brokers, and so on—you need to have good people skills.

These skills include friendliness, openness, kindness, and a genuine interest and liking for all kinds of different people. Keep in mind that everyone has a story—they've experienced joy, pain, and sorrow—and is worthy of respect. Try not to second guess someone's motivations, especially when they create negative consequences for you; most of the time, their rudeness or change of heart has nothing to do with you. However, if you are met repeatedly with similar negative treatment, it may be that you are unintentionally sending the wrong signals. In other words, try not to take things personally, but if you see a pattern emerging, take a hard look at yourself to be sure you aren't at fault.

Listening Skills

Real estate agents need to listen carefully to the needs and desires of their customers, so they can serve those needs and close the sale. Sometimes you need to listen so carefully that you pick up things that are implied but not clearly stated. Your clients may not be able to tell you exactly what they are looking for, so you'll need to pay attention to the clues they give in order to help them find it.

Ability to Learn from Mistakes

Face up to your mistakes and use them to learn the procedures needed for situations that may be similar in the future. For example, after a listing meeting with a seller that you didn't get, make note of what went wrong and why, to help you overcome that obstacle in your next listing meeting.

LEARNING FROM MENTORS

A mentor is someone you identify as successful and with whom you create an informal teacher-student relationship. Choose your mentor based on what is important to you and on how you define success. Someone can be successful without having achieved certain titles or positions, so keep an open mind when you're looking for a mentor. The purpose of having a mentor is to learn from him or her. Enter into the relationship intending to observe your mentor carefully and ask a lot of questions. The following is a list of things you might be able to learn from a mentor:

► Public interaction skills
► Negotiation skills
► What to expect in the workplace culture
► How to communicate with your broker or office manager
► In-depth knowledge about technology and business practices used by your office
► Helpful tips for balancing your work schedule and personal life
► Advice about areas of specialization
► What conferences/classes/training programs you should attend

Finding a Mentor

You'll probably need to actively search for a mentor in your real estate office, unless someone informally decides to take you under his or her wing and show you the ropes. A mentor can be anyone from the broker herself, to one of your peers. There is no formula for who makes a good mentor; it is not based on title, level of seniority, or years in the field. Instead, the qualities of a good mentor are based on a combination of willingness to take on the role, level of expertise in a certain area, teaching ability, and attitude.

There are many ways to find a mentor. Here are a couple of techniques you can try for identifying possible mentors in your office:

► Observe people. You can learn a lot about people by watching them. When asked a question, do they take the time to help you find a resolution or do they point you toward someone else who can help you? The one who takes the time to help you resolve your question is the better choice for a mentor. How does the potential mentor resolve problems? In a calm manner? Do problems get resolved? If so, they are probably a good mentor.
► Listen to people who admire your potential mentor. What is it that people admire about him or her? Do the admirable qualities coincide

with your values and goals? If you need to improve your negotiation skills, you probably shouldn't consider a mentor who is known as cold and unyielding. Instead, look for someone whom people describe as personable, responsive, and who has strong communication skills.

Keep in mind that other real estate sales agents are working on a commission basis, so they may not feel compelled to spend several hours helping you along and giving you tips. Focus on small bites of time, gaining information gradually. You may also want to consider targeting your sponsoring broker or office manager to become a mentor, because they may not only have more time, but also have an interest in your success (your commissions mean money for them, too). Donna Dawson, a sales agent in San Jose, California, remembers:

> When I joined my office seven years ago, my broker helped me connect with an experienced agent who served as a mentor for me. Her assistance and encouragement were very much appreciated. She allowed me to assist her in a number of ways—for example, searching for properties, preparing information for the client, or checking the MLS for updates and status changes.

Don't feel compelled to stick with your mentor(s) forever since career growth may open up new possibilities to you in new areas of specialization. If that happens, you'll probably want to find additional mentors who can show you the ropes in the new environment. However, any former mentors you can keep as friends may not only help you career-wise, but they can also enrich your life in personal ways.

FITTING IN AT THE OFFICE

Some real estate offices have an informal atmosphere, in which everyone jokes with one another and socializes. Other offices are more formal. Although you made an assessment of the work atmosphere while on your job search, you may be in for a few surprises once you've been on the job for a few weeks. It's best to play it safe in the beginning, and assume a more formal tone when interacting with your superiors and coworkers. You can always relax your demeanor after some time on the job to better fit in at a more relaxed office.

If you find the atmosphere in your office is not what you expected, give it some time. It's not necessarily a sign that you're in the wrong place. Newcomers need to pay attention to how business is done, and follow suit. If you're in a highly competitive office, you'll need to keep your leads to yourself, and concentrate on bringing in commissions. Getting along well with coworkers won't be as important to your manager as making a sale.

However, if you find yourself in more relaxed surroundings, in which sales agents help each other out and work as a friendly team, being a team player will be rewarded. An agent working in New York contrasts two different real estate companies:

> The first company that I worked for did not have a friendly and cooperative atmosphere in the office. I found that I began to stay away from the office more and more often. Every time I went into the office and spoke to the other agents, I felt uncomfortable and nervous. Everything was a big competition. The top producing agents acted like they couldn't be bothered with the newcomers and the other new people didn't bond together either because they were competing for the same sales. I knew it was time to move on, so when I found another company that was owned by some friends of my uncle, I jumped at the chance to transfer. I've been there ever since because the atmosphere is totally different. I wanted to work in a fun and friendly office, so I am very relieved to have found one.

INTERACTING WITH THE PUBLIC

Public interaction is an important part of the real estate professional's daily routine; indeed, it is often considered to be the single most important aspect of the job. Positive interactions with buyers, sellers, tenants, and banking professionals will greatly increase your job success.

You might want to consider taking some continuing education courses or one-day seminars in communication skills, public relations, customer service, sales, or public speaking to increase your skills in this critical area. If you have a genuine liking for a variety of people, that natural feeling should shine through and help you out of some potentially rough spots. Inevitably, there will be challenging people and challenging situations that you'll face in your real estate career. The trick is to anticipate and prepare for these challenges ahead of time. Education is one way to help in this regard.

Another big concern when interacting with the public is the topic of agency, which was probably covered in your pre-license course(s). However, any additional information that you can find or read about the topic of agency will help you to perform your duties ethically, legally, and professionally. Historically, most sales agents worked as an agent for the seller, and buyers were left to fend for themselves. Now, many buyers may retain what is commonly referred to as a "buyer's agent" to help them find and purchase their home. You know that several rules apply to the actions an agent can and cannot undertake for the person or people she represents. Never take any actions that could be misconstrued by either party when you are an agent for only one party of an agreement.

USING THE LATEST TECHNOLOGY

The growing use of computers and other technology in the real estate field cannot be ignored. While you don't have to become an expert, you will need to be familiar with the basics. Real estate sales agents we polled noted that just a few years ago, they carried a pen, paper documents, and a key chain. Today, typical salespeople carry Palm Pilots or other electronic organizers, electronic keys, digital cameras, pagers, and cell phones. They also use computers to market their properties and exchange information with clients and their peers. A veteran with over 20 years of sales experience says:

> If you're not comfortable with technology today, you might as well find another field. There is no part of this business that lacks some technological aids, and the array of available real estate-related software is mind-boggling. The only real problem is that now, if you take advantage of every possible technological tool and device, you'll need a wheelbarrow to carry them!

The most basic and most important tool for real estate professionals is the computer. It is your access to the Multiple Listing Service (MLS) program that lists all the homes for sale. While the MLS was once a thick book put out every few weeks, it is now an up-to-the-minute resource that includes prices, length of time on the market, pictures, and most of the other details you'll need to know about a property. In addition to giving you access to this mainstay of the real estate business, there are some other important uses for computers in your business.

IN THE NEWS

For the past decade, REALTORS® have accessed and updated MLS listings through a few different computer programs. Now, the National Association of REALTORS® has recently approved RETS, or Realtor Transactions Standards. RETS is a software platform designed to make it easier to exchange electronic data between different applications. Once it is put into use, real estate professionals will be able to access and update MLS listings (adding pictures and interactive components) faster and easier than before. RETS should be a familiar tool for most REALTORS® within the next few years.

Contact Management Software

One of the secrets to success in a people-oriented field like real estate is to keep track of all your contacts. Traditionally, sales agents who wanted to make a list of contacts would write down applicable information on index cards and store them in a box in their desk. Now, however, you have a wide choice of computer software that you can use to create, update, and manage your list of contacts.

Many contact software programs are called PIMs, or Personal Information Managers. They can be used to organize your time as well as your contacts. Other worthwhile programs include databases (popular ones are part of Microsoft Office and other professional software packages); these are useful in sorting your contact list once you've created it. You can also create a file in a word processing program that has a mail merge feature to create letters, newsletters, postcards, or brochures to send to your contacts on a regular basis without having to type in all those names and addresses each time you want to send out a mailing. Many of these programs are offered for free on real estate websites, so make a point of doing some research before making any purchases.

Whatever method you choose, it is to your advantage use the computer to manage your list of contacts. As you grow in the field, so will your contact list, and your need to keep it organized. Many successful real estate professionals boast of contact lists that exceed 2,500 people!

Using the Internet to Boost Your Success

Your real estate training may have included information on the Internet, or you may have come to the real estate field already familiar with this important tool. If not, it won't take long to catch up, as there is a wealth of information in books, magazines, and classrooms to help you get on the web. Below are listed some helpful books for real estate professionals; other resources are listed in Appendix A.

One Day Course: Real Estate Internet Skills, Curt Robbins (DDC Publishing, Inc., 1999).

Closing the Deal, Leigh Ronald Grossman, ed. (LearningExpress, 2001).

Virtual Reality: A Guide to the Internet for Real Estate and Ancillary Professionals, Lori Robertson, Brian C. Wadell (Hollis Publishing Co., 1996).

Web Marketing for the Real Estate Professional, Bill Koelzer, et al. (Prentice Hall, 2001).

Once you're on the Internet, you'll be able to browse through thousands of sites, such as those set up by national agencies, local brokerages, and individual agents. You can see properties listed by others, and get marketing ideas from other agents. There are countless helpful tips and techniques for success at real estate related websites. The Internet is used by thousands of professionals who are willing to share their knowledge and experience. To find them, use a search engine such as www.lycos.com, and type in search terms such as "real estate."

When you're familiar with the websites of others, you may want to consider launching one of your own, as countless other salespeople have done. Many real estate sites, perhaps including the one run by your employer, will let you set up your own page for free (others charge a nominal fee). If not, check with your Internet service provider (ISP), who probably offers this service to subscribers. Website creation is getting easier all the time, but if you are not comfortable with the idea of creating your own site, there are plenty of people out there who will do it for you. Check the yellow pages or the Internet for local business or individuals who can help you.

On your own website, you should consider including the following:

- ▶ A picture of yourself (professional portraits make a great impression)
- ▶ Contact information (your address, phone number, e-mail address)
- ▶ Information about you and your business (make an impression on potential clients)
- ▶ Pictures of properties you have sold or listed
- ▶ Links to other real estate sites
- ▶ Links to mortgage sites

Using E-mail as a Success Step

As the number of people who own home computers grows, and as the number of people who use e-mail at work grows, so does your opportunity to use e-mail as a communication tool. You can save time by quickly jotting down an answer to a buyer's question or to confirm a meeting with a seller by whisking off a quick e-mail message. You'll find that many of your customers, clients, and prospects rely heavily on e-mail and that they check for e-mail messages several times a day. You may receive e-mail from prospective clients who have viewed your listings or read about your services on the Web. Remember to answer all the mail you receive promptly and professionally; today's prospective client may become tomorrow's satisfied customer.

Many e-mail programs allow attachments to be sent along with the e-mail, so you can attach copies of contracts, listings, and newsletters with your message. Notice if an e-mail address is listed on a business card whenever you receive one, and be sure to include e-mail addresses with your other contact information. Remain alert to comments about computers and e-mail in your conversations to gauge how common their usage is becoming with the people you deal with on a daily basis. If your clients, colleagues, and other contacts are online, take advantage of the fact and use e-mail to keep in touch.

Real Estate Software Programs

Many software companies have developed computer software specifically targeted to real estate professionals. Your employer is probably already using software to manage his or her business, and may expect you to become familiar with your office's system. But if your brokerage offers limited or no access to computer software, you may want to consider purchasing some for yourself. Virtually every aspect of your business can be computerized, from managing contacts to receiving voice mail. Below are listed some examples of types of recently released software programs, all designed to help the real estate professional improve business.

Real Estate Forms (print blank or completed forms)
Calendars and Calculators
Spell-Checkers
Contact List Managers
Lead Managers
Buyer Assistance
Website Design
Direct Mailing/Marketing/Promotional
Desktop Publishing
Financial Analysis (qualify buyers)
Training Courses
Telemarketing

Showings Management
Prospecting
Scheduling
Virtual Property Tours
Property Management
Checkbooks

Whatever position you find yourself in within the real estate field, you'll most likely be able to find some type of computer software to boost your productivity. Becoming adept at working with these programs can give you a big jump on the competition and increase your potential for success.

RENEWING YOUR LICENSE

You'll need to renew your real estate license at regular intervals throughout your career. Renewal times and requirements vary from state to state, but you can find out how to renew your license from your state's real estate commission or licensing agency (see Chapter 3 for contact information). Most states require that you complete a certain number of continuing education credits before you can renew your license. Many times you can complete these credits through self-paced correspondence study, making it less disruptive to your work schedule. Some states allow you to count one-day seminars as a portion of your continuing education credits. Here is an example of what one state requires for renewing a salesperson license:

South Dakota Salesperson License Renewal Requirements

- Renewal must take place every two years
- $100.00 fee
- 24 hours of approved continuing education in any of the following courses:
  (1) Real estate ethics
  (2) Legislative issues that influence real estate practice including both pending and recent legislation

(3) The administration of licensing provisions of real estate law and the rules, including compliance and regulatory practices

(4) Real estate financing, including mortgages and other financing techniques

(5) Real estate market measurement and evaluation, including site evaluations, market data, and feasibility studies

(6) Real estate brokerage administration, including office management, trust accounts, and employee contracts

(7) Real estate mathematics

(8) Real property management, including leasing agreements, accounting procedures, and management contracts

(9) Real property exchange

(10) Land use planning and zoning

(11) Real estate securities and syndication

(12) Estate building and portfolio management

(13) Accounting and taxation as applied to real property

(14) Land development

(15) Real estate appraising

(16) Real estate marketing procedures

(17) The use of calculators or computers as applied to the practice of real estate

(18) Basic computer skills.

Some states send renewal notices in the mail, which may be filled out and mailed back with the required fee and proof of meeting continuing education requirements. If you don't receive a renewal notice in the mail, you may have to renew your license in person at an approved location. Be sure to contact your state licensing board well ahead of your renewal deadline to find out their requirements.

The importance of renewing your license on time cannot be overemphasized. If you forget, or fail to renew on time, your license could be placed on "inactive" status, meaning you must cease all real estate activity for which a license is required, until renewal takes place and active status is restored. (Performing real estate business without a license can result in severe monetary penalties, including the return of commissions earned after your license expired.) Other penalties may include license suspension or revocation. Therefore, it is imperative that you stay informed of your license renewal policies, time frames, and procedures.

ADVANCEMENT OPPORTUNITIES

Some real estate sales agents remain very satisfied with their jobs and offices, and they stay for several years, or even their whole careers, as agents. Others join small real estate offices and then move on to increasingly larger offices. Still others work to become brokers and eventually open their own offices. The advancement route that professionals in real estate pursue is quite different from many other professions, because it depends more on the results of their work and the additional training they pursue than on winning the favor of someone in a management position.

Advancement opportunities for real estate professionals may depend on any one or more of the following factors:

▶ Record as a top producer
▶ Years of experience in the field
▶ Quantity and quality of professional contacts
▶ Availability of management positions in office
▶ Growth of the company
▶ Education level
▶ Management skills

You may have all the qualifications, motivation, and skills needed to become an office manager or broker in your local office, but there may not be any openings available. You can either wait for an opening to occur, or you can apply for a job in another real estate office that has an opening. Or if you pass the broker examination and fulfill all other requirements, you could open your own office or run a branch office of the company for which you're currently working.

You have to determine what is important to you when considering advancement opportunities, so that your career choices will fit into an overall plan. For instance, you might want to transfer to another real estate office—by getting a new job in a different office, you can, in essence, give yourself a promotion. You can get any one or more of the following added benefits from a move:

▶ Higher commission split or lower administrative fees
▶ Better training programs
▶ Better office environment, administrative support, and computer equipment
▶ Better camaraderie with other salespeople and supervisors
▶ Better reputation of real estate company's name
▶ More homes to list and sell, resulting in higher commissions (especially when relocating to a growing area of the country, such as Florida, Arizona, or Nevada, to name a few)

Of course, if you land your first job in a solid real estate office that has a professional and congenial atmosphere, lots of training programs, and a solid reputation, then you're all set. You can focus on learning all you can and applying yourself for future opportunities or career challenges in related areas.

Entering Management

You can climb the ladder to success in real estate by entering management in a large real estate firm. Some of the national franchises as well as the larger independent companies employ many real estate administrators and executives in their headquarters and branch offices. Examples of such positions include manager of a particular specialization in real estate, such as relocation, corporate accounts, advertising, historic homes, commercial properties, foreclosures, and so on, and divisional or regional vice presidents, all the way up to senior vice president.

The best way to break into these management positions is to gain experience and education in an area of real estate that appears to be growing, and/or you are most interested in. Most executives in real estate have a college degree in business, finance, accounting, or real estate. Indeed some hold advanced degrees including the popular MBA degree (master of business administration). However, experienced and savvy professionals who do not have a college degree have also been able to secure high-paying and highly visible executive jobs based on their successful track record in the business.

If you land a job in a large real estate corporation, you may be able to work your way up the career ladder through several promotions in-house. If you don't see such opportunities available in your current company, there's always the option of giving yourself a promotion by seeking a management position in another, larger company. Some management experience or training is usually necessary to land such positions, however, so if you don't possess this background, you may want to consider enrolling in a college degree program or other professional courses. See Chapter 2 for information about real estate education.

Becoming a Broker

If you decide you want to become a real estate broker, begin by checking the licensing requirements listed by state in Chapter 3. These requirements vary from state to state, but generally include some form of the following:

- ▶ Coursework in an approved real estate training program
- ▶ Experience as a sales agent; in some cases, significant education, such as a bachelor's degree in real estate, may be substituted
- ▶ Passing a state licensing exam
- ▶ Getting fingerprinted and passing a background check
- ▶ Becoming a resident in the location you want to become a broker

You may find out that you prefer work as an associate broker under the auspices of a senior broker, continuing to focus on selling real estate. Or you may want to open your own real estate office and hire sales agents to work for you. This option can take significant start-up costs and may take quite a while to realize a profit. Taking some entrepreneurial courses at a local college or university can prove invaluable when deciding whether or not to go this route. You have to weigh the possible benefits against the possible negative outcomes very carefully, as well as examine your own financial standing and ability to get financing for such a venture, before diving in to the process.

Succeeding as a Real Estate Broker/Office Manager/Owner

Gaining management experience and skills will help you to succeed as a sponsoring broker who manages or owns a real estate office. Several options are available for gaining additional management skills. You can take courses at your local community college, enroll in a distance-learning program to earn a bachelor's degree, or join a professional organization and take its self-study courses.

One of the many ways you can achieve greater success as a broker is to obtain a professional designation. These were discussed in Chapter 4, and include the Certified Residential Broker (CRB) designation. In order to achieve it, you must be a member of the National Association of REAL-TORS® and have a minimum of two consecutive years of real estate broker-age management experience. You can take courses on topics such as Managing a Real Estate Business Successfully, Using Management Information Systems Effectively, Managing People for Maximum Productivity, Interactive Decision-Making, and so on.

OTHER CAREERS IN REAL ESTATE

Real estate is a diverse field that offers numerous career choices, whatever your basic interests and abilities may be. In general, training and experience as a residential sales agent offer a good background for other real estate careers. Certain career paths involve returning to college or even graduate school for more in-depth study of subjects, such as finance and insurance, only touched on by the basic real estate pre-license course(s). There are also entry-level career paths in jobs closely related to the real estate field, such as title researcher and mortgage broker, which have specific education or certification requirements, but don't necessarily require real estate sales training.

To get an idea of the possibilities open to you, read the following job descriptions of key career opportunities that are either a specialization in the real estate field or are in a closely related field.

Real Estate Appraiser

Real estate appraisers estimate the market value of properties. They investigate the quality of construction, the overall condition of the property, and its functional design. They gather information by taking measurements, interviewing persons familiar with the property's history, and searching public records of sales, leases, assessments, and other transactions. A real estate appraiser in Las Vegas, Nevada shares her experience:

> The fact that I was being entrusted to come up with a value for a home made me feel great when I first got into this business. It was a little nerve-racking at first, but I learned a lot from my mentor. She had been in the business for several years and was a veteran. I followed her around and studied every move she made until I felt comfortable with the whole process. It's a great thing to be able to provide this service because not that many people know how to do it.

Appraisers may compare a property with other similar properties for which recent sale prices or rental data are available to help them arrive at an estimate of value. In other cases, appraisers estimate the costs of reproducing the structure on the property, add that to the value of the land, and then combine that information with how much the value of the existing structure has depreciated. For rental properties, an appraiser may estimate the current and future income generated by the rental of the property to determine its current value.

Appraisers, therefore, spend a lot of time outside of their offices conducting research to determine a property's value. They need to possess strong research, organization, and math skills and should also be detail oriented. They may also need to understand blueprints and survey drawings. Appraisers normally devote a portion of their monthly work schedule to keeping up with the latest government regulations and economic trends both nationally and in their local region.

Several changes occurred in the appraisal industry resulting from Title XI of the federal legislation entitled Financial Institutions Reform, Recovery, and Enforcement Act of 1989 (FIRREA), which is currently being studied in anticipation of legislating tighter regulations. The 1989 legislation requires appraisers to be state licensed or certified in order to conduct federally related real estate transactions and to follow the Uniform Standards of Professional Appraisal Practice (USPAP). Because the professional standards are constantly changing, appraisers who work on federal projects continually seek information about the changes and regulations to remain up-to-date.

The 1989 Initiative mandated a more thorough appraisal than had previously been allowed. It required the appraiser to complete a new three-page form describing the physical condition of a home in unprecedented detail. HUD will give appraisers a handbook explaining the new appraisal standards. (You can find the handbook online at: www.hud.gov/reac/reasfappr.html.) Log on to one of the national appraisers' association websites, such as www.appraisalinstitute.org to read about new legislation that may affect this field.

Many appraisers choose to specialize in one area, so they can increase their knowledge and expertise in that area and gain a reputation in one particular specialization, such as single-family homes, multiple-family homes, apartment complexes, condominiums, commercial property, public housing, or some other niche market. The services of real estate appraisers may be required by any of the following:

▶ Banks
▶ Mortgage lenders
▶ Investors
▶ Home buyers
▶ Home sellers
▶ Insurance companies
▶ Developers
▶ Corporations
▶ Tax assessor's office

Several job opportunities exist for real estate appraisers with government agencies, large real estate offices, banks, insurance companies, tax assessor firms, and appraiser consulting firms, in addition to becoming self-employed.

Professional Designations

A key to success in appraisal is to earn one or more professional designations. We discussed these designations as they related to sales agents and brokers in Chapter 2. The designations available to appraisers are similar, in that they are offered through associations, and involve education and other criteria set by the association. Once awarded, they allow the appraiser to use the letters of the designation after his or her name, indicating to the public a commitment to the profession, and desire to remain on top of the changes in the field of appraisal. Appraiser designations are offered by a number of organizations, including:

- ▶ The Appraisal Institute
- ▶ American Society of Appraisers
- ▶ American Society of Farm Managers and Rural Appraisers
- ▶ International Association of Assessing Officers
- ▶ International Right of Way Association
- ▶ National Association of Independent Fee Appraisers

See Appendix B for contact information for these associations.

The Appraisal Institute confers a general designation, the MAI (Member of Appraisal Institute), and a residential designation, the SRA (Senior Residential Appraiser). These professionals must adhere to a strictly enforced code of professional ethics and standards of appraisal practice, and have a four-year college degree, in addition to other requirements. The basic level MAI must complete 172 hours of coursework; Appraisal Principles (39 hours), Appraisal Procedures (39 hours), Basic Income Capitalization (39 hours), General Applications (39 hours), and Standards of Professional Practice, Part A (USPAP) (16 hours). To achieve level two, an appraiser must take an additional 211 hours in Standards of Professional Practice, Part B (11 hours), Advanced Income Capitalization (40 hours), Highest & Best Use and Market Analysis (40 hours), Advanced Sales Comparison and Cost Approaches (40 hours), Report Writing and Valuation Analysis (40 hours), and Advanced Applications (40 hours).

The Appraisal Institute's basic level SRA must complete 133 hours of coursework in Appraisal Principles (39 hours), Appraisal Procedures (39 hours), Residential Case Study (39 hours), and Standards of Professional

Practice, Part A (USPAP) (16 hours). The second level requires an additional 40 hours in two advanced real estate courses.

Another professional association that offers an appraisal designation is the American Society of Appraisers. Every designated appraiser must start his or her ASA membership as a candidate member. With additional experience and qualifications, you can become an accredited member and then an accredited senior appraiser. Requirements for becoming a candidate member include having a four-year college degree, two years of experience in appraising, passing the ASA's ethics exam, and passing an exam on the Uniform Standards of Professional Appraisal Practice (USPAP) within a specified period of time. The accredited member and senior appraiser require additional experience and education.

IN THE NEWS

The Department of Housing and Urban Development (HUD) has enacted a new Homebuyer Protection Initiative. HUD has increased the scope of appraisals and the responsibility and liability of appraisers who participate in the over 1,000,000, Federal Housing Authority (FHA) assignments annually (new home purchases only). (FHA is part of HUD.) HUD's intention to "strongly urge homebuyers to get home inspections in addition to an appraisal," will increase demand for home inspections. HUD's blessings further legitimize the industry and may finally lead to acceptance of the notion, by lenders and homebuyers, that home inspections are vital and should be a routine part of every real estate transaction.

Requirements for Appraisers

The trend is for prospective appraisers to graduate from college with a degree in business administration, real estate, finance, or a related field and then start their career by becoming a trainee and working with an experienced appraiser for several months to a year or more. Historically, many appraisers without a college degree came into the field from another real estate specialty, such as sales or brokerage, and some appraisers still enter the field that way today.

All appraisers must be state licensed, just as real estate sales agents and brokers must be (see Appendix B for a list of state licensing agencies). The federal government has been instituting tighter restrictions and stricter certification requirements for appraisers who perform work for the federal government. Indeed, real estate appraisers must not only be licensed but also certified as well, in order to appraise certain types of federally related real estate transactions.

Income for Appraisers

In direct contrast to real estate sales agents and brokers, real estate appraisers do not receive commissions based on the value of the property they assess. In fact, it is against the law for appraisers to get this type of a commission—the appraiser needs to be accurate and honest, and free from any temptation to inflate the value of a property in order to increase his or her own income. Most appraisers are paid a flat fee for each project, and many appraisers are self-employed. Others may work for an appraisal consulting firm or other organization and receive a set salary or a commission based on the number of projects completed. The standard flat fee for appraising a home is approximately $200–$300. Of course, that fee may be higher or lower in certain parts of the country or for certain homes that require more complex appraisals.

Property Manager

A real estate property manager's responsibilities range from living on-site and collecting rent in an apartment complex to managing several on-site managers from a remote location. Property managers may be responsible for maintaining commercial or residential real estate, or both, depending on the size and expertise of the property management firm. Some firms are one-person operations that consist of a self-employed property manager. Others may be large corporations that employ hundreds of property managers and administrative workers who handle the paperwork involved in property management.

The responsibilities of property managers vary depending on the type of property they are managing, the number of properties they are managing, and the relationship they have to the owner(s) of the property. Many property managers work on-site. That is, they live on the premises of the property they manage, such as apartment complexes, condominiums, and multi-family homes. They take care of collecting the rent and negotiating contracts for services such as security, cleaning crews, landscapers, trash collectors, and repair workers. Obviously, the complexity of this job ranges a great deal depending on the type and size of the property that is being managed. Many other property managers do not live on-site, but they manage a large number of the daily operations from an off-site location, perhaps for several different properties.

In addition to managing the daily operations of a property, many property managers need to be well versed in applicable laws, tax regulations, and other administrative knowledge. They need to be aware of local and national housing laws, such as the Americans with Disabilities Act and the Federal Fair Housing Amendment Act. Many property managers also complete detailed reports regarding the property's income and expenses for submission to the owner. They also often show rental properties and explain the lease terms and property regulations to prospective tenants.

Many property managers specialize in one or more of the following areas:

▶ Single-family homes
▶ Two to six family homes (also known as duplexes, triplexes, six-plexes, etc.)
▶ Apartment complexes
▶ Condominiums
▶ Homeowner associations
▶ Asset manager
▶ Land development

One way to break into this field is to take a property or asset management internship. Many companies offer these to college students or those already in the work force, as a way to see first-hand the work of property management. Some internships are paid, offering hourly wages, while others earn college credits. Most are for a specified, short period of time, such as four to twelve weeks. Search the Internet using the terms "property management" and "internship" to see many listings. Some of the associations listed below also have internship listings on their websites.

Asset Managers

Some property managers purchase, develop, and sell properties for individual and business investors. They may be known as asset managers, as there is a recent trend making a distinction between the two groups. Professional associations, such as the American Society of Asset Managers, encourage this trend. Property managers who manage assets perform long-term strategic financial planning and have an overview of the financial aspects of each deal instead of focusing on the daily operations of the property. They need to be familiar with several real estate principles in order to make the best decision on whether to buy or sell a particular property. Some of these issues may include:

▶ Property value
▶ Tax rates
▶ Population growth
▶ Zoning regulations
▶ Traffic patterns and volume
▶ Mortgage terms
▶ Creative financing

Land Development Managers

Another area of specialization for property managers is to work for land development companies. These property managers acquire land and plan the construction of commercial buildings on that land. This is a complex job. Land development managers interact with several different people to bring a construction project to fruition. They spend a great deal of time negotiating with professionals in various local, state, or federal government offices, public utilities, community organizations, finance companies, mortgage lenders, architectural and design firms, construction companies, lobbying groups, and other businesses.

Professional Designations and Certifications

One of the ways you can increase your marketability and chances for a top job as a professional property manager is to earn professional designations or certifications from professional associations. Here are some of the associations that offer continuing education or professional designations to property managers:

▶ Institute of Real Estate Management
▶ Building Owners and Managers Association International
▶ Community Associations Institute
▶ National Apartment Association
▶ National Association of Residential Property Managers
▶ National Association of Home Builders
▶ National Property Management Association, Inc.

See Appendix B for contact information for these associations.

The National Property Management Association, Inc. offers the following certifications: Certified Professional Property Specialist (CPPS), Certified Professional Property Administrator (CPPA), and Certified Professional Property Manager (CPPM). To achieve the CPPS level, no work experience is required. For the CPPA, you must document at least three years of work experience, and for the CPPM, at least six years. In addition, the CPPM level requires at least four years of supervisory or decision-making positions: management of personnel, projects, or budgets qualifies. For all three certifications, there are comprehensive tests on Contracts, Federal, and Standard Property Management issues.

The Institute of Real Estate Management also offers professional designations to property and asset managers. To earn the Certified Property Manager (CPM) designation, you need to demonstrate a certain amount of property management experience and complete several real estate related courses. They also offer the Accredited Residential Manager (ARM) designation for professionals who specialize in managing residential properties.

Other professional designations may have similar requirements. Check with each professional association to find out what benefits they offer their members and read all membership application materials carefully before joining any association.

Requirements for Property Managers

The typical minimum requirements for becoming a property manager vary depending on the type of property management you want to do. Many managers enter the field by gaining work experience as an on-site manager at an apartment complex, condominium, or homeowner association or as an assistant manager in a large property management company. Many prospective property managers attend or graduate from college to land entry-level management jobs in the field, although a college degree is not required for all property management jobs. However, if you want to specialize in asset management or land development, you'll probably need either significant experience in the field or a high level of training, such as a bachelor's degree in real estate, finance, or management. Indeed, many more large employers are now requiring entry-level property managers to hold a college degree in business administration, real estate, or a related field. (See the sample job postings on page 156, taken from recent help wanted advertisements, for an idea as to what employers are looking for.)

Typical Income Level

Income levels vary depending on the type, size, and location of properties that are managed, as well as the area of specialization that a property manager is in. The average annual earnings for property managers were $9,930 in 1998, while the top ten percent of property managers earned more than $74,500, according to the Bureau of Labor Statistics. Almost one half were self-employed, three times the average for all executive, administrative, and managerial occupations. Many managers receive a percentage of the rent that is generated from the properties they manage. Several on-site managers receive an apartment to live in rent-free as a part of their compensation. Property managers who specialize in land development property management often receive a small percentage of the profits from the properties they develop, or get some of the land itself.

Mortgage Broker/Mortgage Banker

Mortgage brokers and bankers provide an essential service to real estate buyers. Without the help of these financing specialists, many deals would not go through. Therefore, this field is an integral part of the real estate business. Mortgage brokers and bankers help to match up potential buyers with lenders who will give those buyers a satisfactory mortgage. There is an important distinction between the scope of professional activity of mortgage brokers and bankers. Mortgage bankers not only help buyers to get a loan, they also service that loan. That is, they collect the monthly payments from the buyers, make sure that appropriate taxes and insurance fees are paid, and may ascertain whether the property is suitably maintained. Mortgage brokers do not get involved in servicing the loans that they help borrowers to obtain. Their primary objective is to match up real estate buyers with lenders and get those loans closed.

Most mortgage bankers and brokers not only bring borrowers and lenders together, they also help the buyers through each step of the loan process. This may include helping the borrowers fill out complex loan application forms and giving them updated information about each step of the loan application process. They also will often coordinate getting the property appraised or inspected as required by the lender and making sure all legal requirements are met by both sides of all loan transactions.

Mortgage brokers and bankers work with several different lending institutions to ensure that they obtain the best loan possible for each buyer that they work with. They may work with anywhere from four to thirteen different lenders at any one given time. They need to be very familiar with each lender's financing terms and related costs. Many areas of specialization exist in larger mortgage brokerage firms due to the breadth and depth of knowledge needed in this field. Some areas of specialization include:

- ▶ Loan Solicitors
- ▶ Loan Underwriters
- ▶ Loan Processors
- ▶ Office Managers
- ▶ Mortgage Sellers
- ▶ Commercial Mortgage Specialists

The careers of mortgage brokers and bankers are relatively new in the real estate field; indeed, they have grown significantly over the last decade.

Real Estate Developer

Real estate developers face the challenge of turning empty land or decaying buildings into thriving, profitable residential or commercial developments.

They spend a considerable amount of time and money conducting research on site selection. They must thoroughly understand the site, the site's potential, the site's surrounding neighborhood, and the future possibilities for the neighboring land. After selecting an appropriate site for development, developers then analyze the projected costs and work on getting the project financed. They must then secure adequate financing, hire contractors, and oversee them as they construct the buildings on the site. Once the buildings are finished, the developers oversee the management, marketing, or sale of the final property.

Real Estate Instructor

Real estate agents or brokers who are interested in teaching may wish to become instructors at a private school, a nearby college or university, or other real estate training school. Instructors provide training to all levels of real estate agents, from new recruits to agents who need to fulfill continuing education requirements. In addition to performing as instructors in a classroom, they may also organize or update training programs for specific groups of people. For example, a real estate office may want to contract out to an instructor, a particular seminar on a hot topic, such as buyer agency. You then might be asked to come in-house to conduct a seminar on the topic. (See the sample job postings on page 156 for an example, taken from a recent help-wanted ad.)

Title Searcher

Title searchers play an important role in real estate transactions. They conduct searches to find legal documents pertaining to property titles, such as mortgages, assessments, and deeds. They read the documents they find during their search and compare legal descriptions of the property in question. They often verify deeds of ownership and descriptions of property boundaries. They communicate often with various offices and agencies, including county surveyors, real estate agents, courthouse staff, lenders, buyers, sellers, and others to obtain the information necessary in their search. Title searchers may also examine individual titles and write reports showing any restrictions to the title along with giving information about how the restrictions may be removed. They need to be detail-oriented with strong research and communication skills.

Real Estate Syndication Professional

Real estate syndication professionals are involved in the investment world. They bring people together to invest in properties as a group. Due to the investment portion of their jobs, syndication professionals need to have extensive experience and education in finance. Many syndication professionals enter the field through real estate sales or property management. They need to have strong communication and persuasion skills when addressing groups of people to invest in partnerships that they have set up. A strong background in general business skills and investing would prove helpful for this career.

Real Estate Auctioneer

If you enjoy the high-energy atmosphere in an auction house, you might want to explore the career of real estate auctioneer. These real estate professionals conduct auctions to sell real estate ranging from single-family homes to shopping centers. It can be challenging to land a job in this exciting area of real estate, but you can gain more information about auctioning by attending an auction school, or talking to auctioneers in your local area. The job has increased in popularity within the past several years due to the need for selling foreclosure properties. Many real estate auctioneers own their own companies, and others work for large auction houses either as employees or as independent contractors. Many of the properties that are sold at auctions come from government agencies and are considered distressed properties (ones that may not sell in the traditional method).

SAMPLE JOB POSTINGS

These sample job postings can give you an idea of what type of requirements and pay level are available when seeking new challenges in real estate or related fields. Of course, job duties, commissions, and salaries vary considerably, but these sample postings culled from a variety of sources can give you an idea of the possibilities that are out there.

Position:	Property Management Training Coordinator
Location:	Parsippany, New Jersey
Requirements:	Qualified candidates must possess five years experience, a four-year college degree, and strong PC skills. Corporate training experience is a plus.
Description:	Position requires individual who will manage corporate training programs in Property Management, including development of course materials, booking of speakers, work with multi-media production of courses.
Salary:	$50,000–$55,000 dependent upon qualifications and experience

Position:	Real Estate Portfolio Manager
Location:	Detroit, Michigan
Requirements:	Requires prior commercial real estate and financial analyst experience, with degree in Business or Finance.
Description:	Will develop & systematize database reports for monitoring financial and operational performance of the operators of the company's core portfolio. Areas of review include property level financial statement analysis, operator/guarantor credit analysis, real and personal property tax compliance, insurance compliance, property inspection documentation and letters of credit review.
Salary:	$60,000–$70,000

Position:	Senior Asset Manager
Location:	Portland, Oregon

Requirements:	Prefer at least five years experience in asset or property management, and/or real estate investment analysis; or a Master's degree in Business Administration or related field.
Description:	Manage other asset managers and an assigned portfolio of properties; determine business requirements of partnership agreement; perform variance analysis; analyze property budgets and operating results; monitor cash flow and report property results to investors.
Salary:	$40,000–$50,000

Position:	Regional Real Estate Manager
Location:	Chicago, Illinois
Requirements:	Must have four-year college degree, and at least three years of real estate experience. Must possess strong organizational and communication skills.
Description:	Manages national company's real estate deals throughout Midwest; works with Corporate Real Estate team of planners, architects, and property managers; negotiates real estate leases; contracts for the sale and purchase of property; collects commissions.
Salary:	$58,900–$88,300

ACHIEVING SUCCESS

After you close your first sale as a real estate sales agent, complete your first property appraisal, or manage your first property, you will have begun what promises to be a gratifying and rewarding career. Whether you decide to stay in your first real estate job, or move into a related area within the real estate field, you can be proud to be a part of a necessary and important profession. Pursue each step of your real estate career with diligence, perseverance, and commitment to excellence, and you will be well on your way to achieving great success.

THE INSIDE TRACK

Who: Donna Dawson

What: Sales Agent

Where: Century 21 Seville-Contempo, San Jose, California

How long: Seven years

INSIDER'S STORY

About seven years ago, I was teaching full-time, and looking for different possibilities for a career change. I spoke with many people during my "exploration" phase, and during that time began having conversation with a colleague who was selling real estate as a part-time job. He gave me his broker's name, and I called and arranged an interview.

During the interview, I realized that a career in real estate would be a wonderful opportunity for me to pursue a different line of work, while capitalizing on all of the skills I developed during my career as a teacher. When I first began working as an agent, I teamed up with another new agent in the office. We thought partnering would be a good way to utilize our different strengths—I had many, many contacts from years of residency and employment in the area, as well as from community service activities, plus, the people skills that make meeting with clients and making contacts easy. She had the computer and organizational skills. Unfortunately, our partnership lasted less than a year. The problem was our motivations: I was willing to ease into the career part-time, while still teaching, and she was relying on commissions as her bread and butter. I've worked independently ever since.

There have been many changes in our industry over the years I have worked as an agent. Technology—with the computer and Internet—has certainly changed the way we do business. As our clientele changes, we have to also. Many buyers are surfing the Internet looking for properties before they come into the office, so you need to check the listings on the computer, too. Another change has been the market here in California, which is now what we refer to as "inflated." The inventory of properties is low, while the number of buyers who are financially able to purchase continues to grow, causing prices to go much higher than they would otherwise. Our office has gone so far as to require both seller and buyer to sign a disclosure form stating that they realize that market conditions may have caused them to pay more for a house than they might have in a more stable market. We also advise buyers to consult a financial advisor to help them understand the implications of a purchase under such conditions. The higher number of buyers has also caused a rise in "as-is" sales—buyers are so eager to purchase a property that they are willing to buy it no matter the condition.

INSIDER'S ADVICE

I love selling real estate, and encourage others to enter the profession. Understand the downsides of the job, though. Evening and weekend work is just part of the territory. We have to be available to our clients, or they will find someone else to do the job. You should also develop a business plan that includes systematic and focused marketing, and be sure you are familiar with all of the technology that is a routine part of this business. Contact management computer programs are especially vital. Think about having a website developed, too. Many top producers have their own site, and it can help you build a presence within the real estate community.

Appendix A

Additional Resources

CAREER GUIDES (GENERAL AND REAL ESTATE)

General

Ferguson Staff, Editor. *Encyclopedia of Careers and Vocational Guidance, 11th Edition*. Ferguson Publishing. 1999

U.S. Department of Labor. *Occupational Outlook Handbook 2000–2001*. Jist Works. 2000.

Vgm Career Horizons, Editor. *Vgm's Careers Encyclopedia: A Concise, Up-To-Date Reference for Students, Parents & Guidance Counselors, 4th Edition*. Vgm Career Horizons. 1997.

Real Estate

Clark, Betty. *Choosing a Career in Real Estate*. Rosen Publishing Group. 2001.

Cross, Carla. *On Track to Success in 30 Days: Energize Your Real Estate Career to Become a Top Producer*. Real Estate Education Company. 1996.

Edwards, Kenneth W. *Your Successful Real Estate Career*. AMACOM. 1997.

Evans, Mariwyn. *Opportunities in Real Estate Careers*. Vgm Career Horizons. 1997.

Grossman, Leigh Ronald. *Closing the Deal*. LearningExpress. 2001.

Rathegeber, David. *Agents Guide to Real Estate*. Realty Research Group. 1999.

COLLEGE GUIDES

The College Board. *College Handbook, 38th Ed, 2001*. Henry Holt. 2000.

Franek, Robert, et al. *Best 331 Colleges: 2001 Edition*. Princeton Review. 2000.

Franek, Robert and Julie Mandelbaum (Editors). *Complete Book of Colleges 2001*. Princeton Review. 2000.

Peterson's Guides (Editor). *Peterson's Four-Year Colleges 2001*. Peterson's Guides. 2000.

Peterson's (Editor). *Peterson's Vocational and Technical Schools: East*. Peterson's Guides. 1999.

Peterson's Guides (Editor). *Peterson's Vocational and Technical Schools: West*. Peterson's Guides. 1999.

RESUMES AND INTERVIEWS

Block, Jay A. and Michael Betrus. *101 Best Cover Letters*. McGraw-Hill Professional Publishing. 1999.

Dermott, Brigit (Editor). *The Complete Professional*. LearningExpress. 2000.

Eyre, Vivian V. *Great Interview: Successful Strategies for Getting Hired*. LearningExpress. 2000.

Rich, Jason R. *Great Resume: Get Noticed, Get Hired*. LearningExpress. 2000.

JOB HUNTING

Ackley, Kristina M. *100 Top Internet Job Sites: Get Wired, Get Hired in Today's New Job Market*. Impact Publications. 2000.

Bolles, Richard Nelson. *Job-Hunting on the Internet*. Ten Speed Press. 1999.

———. *What Color Is Your Parachute? 2001: A Practical Manual for Job-Hunters and Career-Changers*. Ten Speed Press. 2000.

Hansen, Katharine. *A Foot in the Door: Networking Your Way into the Hidden Job Market*. Ten Speed Press. 2000.

Mangum, William T. *99 Minutes to Your Ideal Job*. John Wiley & Sons. 1995.

Nierenberg, Andrea. *40 Minutes to Great Networking Skills.* The Nierenberg Group, Inc. 1998.

Shelly, Susan. *Networking for Novices.* LearningExpress. 1998.

REAL ESTATE REFERENCE

Arnold, Alvin L., et al. *The Arnold Encyclopedia of Real Estate, 2nd Edition.* John Wiley & Sons. 1993.

Irwin, Robert, et al. *The 90 Second Lawyer Guide to Buying Real Estate.* John Wiley & Sons. 1997.

Ritchie, John C. *The 3Ps of Negotiating: Exploring the Dimensions.* Prentice Hall. 2000.

REAL ESTATE APPRAISAL

Betts, Richard M. and Silas J. Ely. *Basic Real Estate Appraisal.* Prentice Hall. 1997.

Parnham, Phil and Chris Rispin. *Residential Property Appraisal.* E & FN Spon. 2001.

Ventolo, William L., et al. *Fundamentals of Real Estate Appraisal, 7th Edition.* Real Estate Education Company. 1992.

REAL ESTATE MARKETING

Kennedy, Steve and Deborah Johnson. *2001 Winning Ads for Real Estate.* Argyle Press. 1995.

Martin, Ruth. *The Ruth Martin Story: How to Market Yourself and Sell 100 Houses Every Year.* Celo Valley Books.

Pivar, William and Bradley A. Pivar. *The Big Book of Real Estate Ads: 1001 Ads That Sell.* Real Estate Education Company. 1997.

Stefaniak, Norbert J. *Real Estate Marketing: Develop a Professional Career.* Walker-Pearse, Ltd. 1998.

REAL ESTATE LAW, FINANCE, AND MATH

Armbrust, Betty J., et al. *Practical Real Estate Math*. Holcomb Hathaway. 1995

Coleman, David S., et al. *Real Estate Math: Explanations, Problems, Solutions*. Real Estate Education Company. 1997.

Gadow, Sandy. *All About Escrow and Real Estate Closings: Or How to Buy the Brooklyn Bridge and Have the Last Laugh! 4th Edition*. Escrow Publishing. 1999.

Good-Garton, Julie. *All About Mortgages: Insider Tips for Financing and Refinancing Your Home*. Dearborn Publishing. 1999.

Karp, James. *Real Estate Law, 4th Ed*. Real Estate Education Company. 1998.

REAL ESTATE PROPERTY MANAGEMENT

Baird, Floyd M., et al. *Property Management, 6th Edition*. Real Estate Education Company. 1999.

Evans, Mariwyn and Michael B. Simmons. *Opportunities in Property Management Careers*. NTC/Contemporary Publishing Co. 2000.

REAL ESTATE SALES AND MANAGEMENT

Tuccillo, John A. *The Eight New Rules of Real Estate: Doing Business in a Consumer-Centric, Techno-Savvy World*. Real Estate Education Company. 1999.

Cyr, John E., et al. *Real Estate Brokerage: A Management Guide*. Real Estate Education Company. 1999.

Real Estate Brokerage Managers Council. *Real Estate Office Management*. Real Estate Education Company. 1996.

Galaty, Fillmore, et al. *Modern Real Estate Practice, 15th Edition*. Real Estate Education Company. 1999.

REAL ESTATE TEST PREPARATION

AMP Real Estate Sales Exam. LearningExpress. 1998.

ASI Real Estate Sales Exam. LearningExpress. 1998.

California Real Estate Sales Exam. LearningExpress. 1999.

Gaines, George, Jr., et al. *Florida Real Estate Exam Manual.* Dearborn Trade. 2000.

Meyers, Judith N. *The Secrets of Taking any Test, 2nd Edition.* LearningExpress. 2000.

PSI Real Estate Sales Exam. LearningExpress. 1998.

Texas Real Estate Sales Exam, 2nd Edition. LearningExpress. 2000.

REAL ESTATE JOB WEBSITES

www.architectjobs.com

www.appraiserjobs.com

www.assetmanagerjobs.com

www.facilitymanagerjobs.com

www.ired.com

www.leasingjobs.com

www.maintenanceemployment.com

www.newhomesalesjobs.com

www.propertymanagerjobs.com

www.realestatefinancejobs.com

www.realestatejobstore.com

www.realestatemanagerjobs.com

www.realestatesalesjobs.com

www.realtor.com

www.restatecareer.com

www.superintendentjobs.com

www.titleinsurancejobs.com

Appendix B

State Agencies (Higher Education and Appraisal Licensing), Professional Associations, Educational Accrediting Agencies

STATE HIGHER EDUCATION AGENCIES

ALABAMA
Alabama Commission on Higher Education
100 North Union Street
P.O. Box 302000
Montgomery, AL 36130-2000
334-242-2276

ALASKA
Alaska Commission on Post-secondary
Education
3030 Vintage Boulevard
Juneau, AK 99801-7109
907-465-6741
Fax: 907-465-5316

ARIZONA
Arizona Commission for Post-secondary
Education
2020 North Central Avenue, Suite 275
Phoenix, AZ 85004-4503
602-229-2591
Fax: 602-229-2599
Website: www.acpe.asu.edu

ARKANSAS
Arkansas Department of Education
4 State Capitol Mall, Room 107A
Little Rock, AR 72201-1071
501-682-4396
E-mail: finaid@adhe.arknet.edu

CALIFORNIA
California Student Aid Commission
P.O. Box 419026
Rancho Cordova, CA 95741-9026
Customer Service Department: 916-526-7590
Fax: 916-323-2619

COLORADO
Colorado Commission on Higher Education
Colorado Heritage Center
1300 Broadway, 2nd Floor
Denver, CO 80203
303-866-2723
Fax: 303-860-9750

CONNECTICUT
Connecticut Department of Higher
Education
61 Woodland Street
Hartford, CT 06105-2326
860-947-1855
Fax: 860-947-1311

DELAWARE
Delaware Higher Education Commission
Carvel State Office Building, Fourth Floor
820 North French Street
Wilmington, DE 19801
302-577-3240
Fax: 302-577-6765

DISTRICT OF COLUMBIA
Department of Human Services
Office of Postsecondary Education
Research and Assistance
2100 Martin Luther King Jr. Avenue SE
Suite 401
Washington, D.C. 20020
202-727-3688
Fax: 202-727-2739

FLORIDA
Florida Department of Education
Office of Student Financial Assistance
1344 Florida Education Center
325 West Gaines Street
Tallahassee, FL 32399-0400
888-827-2004
Fax: 850-488-3612

GEORGIA
Georgia Student Finance Commission
2082 East Exchange Place, Suite 100
Tucker, GA 30084
770-724-9030
www.gsfc.org

HAWAII
Hawaii State Post-secondary Education
Commission
2444 Dole Street, Room 209
Honolulu, HI 96822-2394
808-956-8207
Fax: 808-956-5156

IDAHO
Idaho State Board of Education
P.O. Box 83720
Boise, ID 83720-0037
208-334-2270
Fax: 208-334-2632

ILLINOIS
Illinois Student Assistance Commission
(ISAC)
1755 Lake Cook Road
Deerfield, IL 60015-5209
800-899-4722
www.isac-online.org

INDIANA
State Student Assistance Commission of
Indiana
150 West Market Street, Suite 500
Indianapolis, IN 46204-2811
317-232-2350
Fax: 317-232-3260

IOWA
Iowa College Student Aid Commission
200 10th Street, 4th Floor
Des Moines, IA 50309-3609
515-281-3501
E-mail: csac@max.state.ia.us
www.iowacollegeaid.org

KANSAS
Kansas Board of Regents
700 S.W. Harrison, Suite 1410
Topeka, KS 66603-3760
785-296-3517
Fax: 785-296-0983
E-mail: christy@kbor.state.ks.us
www.ukans.edu/~kbor

KENTUCKY
Kentucky Higher Education Assistance
Authority (KHEAA)
1050 U.S. 127 South
Frankfort, KY 40601-4323
800-928-8926
Fax: 502-696-7345
E-mail: Webmaster@kheaa.com
www.kheaa.com

LOUISIANA

Louisiana Office of Student Financial
Assistance
P.O. Box 91202
Baton Rouge, LA 70821-9202
800-259-5626 ext. 1012
225-922-1012
Fax: 225-922-1089
E-mail:
custserv@osfa.state.la.us or
webmaster@osfa.state.la.us
www.osfa.state.la.us

MAINE

Finance Authority of Maine
P.O. Box 949
Augusta, ME 04332-0949
800-228-3734
207-623-3263
Fax: 207-626-8208
TDD: 207-626-2717
E-mail: info@famemaine.com

MARYLAND

Maryland Higher Education Commission
Jeffrey Building, 16 Francis Street
Annapolis, MD 21401-1781
410-974-5370
Fax: 410-974-5994

MASSACHUSETTS

Massachusetts Board of Higher Education
Office of Student Financial Assistance
330 Stuart Street, 3rd Floor
Boston, MA 02116
617-727-1205
Fax: 617-727-0667

MICHIGAN

Michigan Higher Education Assistance
Authority
Office of Scholarships and Grants
P.O. Box 30462
Lansing, MI 48909-7962
517-373-3394
Fax: 517-335-5984

MINNESOTA

Minnesota Higher Education Services Office
1450 Energy Park Drive, Suite 350
St. Paul, MN 55108-5227
800-657-3866
651-642-0567
www.mheso.state.mn.us

MISSISSIPPI

Mississippi Post-secondary Education
Financial Assistance Board
3825 Ridgewood Road
Jackson, MS 39211-6453
601-982-6663
Fax: 601-982-6527

MISSOURI

Missouri Student Assistance Resource
Services (MOSTARS)
3515 Amazonas Drive
Jefferson City, MO 65109-5717
800-473-6757
573-751-3940
Fax: 573-751-6635
www.mocbhe.gov/mostars/finmenu.htm

MONTANA

Office of Commissioner of Higher Education
Montana Guaranteed Student Loan Program
P.O. Box 203101
Helena, MT 59620-3101
800-537-7508
E-mail: scholars@mgslp.state.mt.us
www.mgslp.state.mt.us

NEBRASKA

Coordinating Commission for Post-secondary Education
P.O. Box 95005
Lincoln, NE 68509-5005
402-471-2847
Fax: 402-471-2886
www.nol.org/NEpostsecondaryed

NEVADA
Nevada Department of Education
700 East Fifth Street
Carson City, NV 89701-5096
775-687-9200
Fax: 775-687-9101

NEW HAMPSHIRE
Post-secondary Education Commission
2 Industrial Park Drive
Concord, NH 03301-8512
603-271-2555
Fax: 603-271-2696
E-mail Address: jknapp@nhsa.state.nh.us
www.state.nh.us

NEW JERSEY
Higher Education Student Assistance
Authority
P.O. Box 540
Trenton, NJ 08625
800-792-8670
Fax: 609-588-3316
www.state.nj.us/treasury/osa

NEW MEXICO
New Mexico Commission on Higher
Education
1068 Cerrillos Road
Santa Fe, NM 87501
800-279-9777
E-mail Address: highered@che.state.nm.us
www.nmche.org

NEW YORK
New York State Higher Education Services
Corporation
One Commerce Plaza
Albany, NY 12255
888-697-4372
Fax: 518-473-3749

NORTH CAROLINA
North Carolina State Education Assistance
Authority
P.O. Box 13663
Research Triangle Park, NC 27709-3663
800-700-1775
E-mail: information@ncseaa.edu

NORTH DAKOTA
North Dakota University System
North Dakota Student Financial Assistance
Program
600 East Boulevard Avenue, Department 215
Bismarck, ND 58505-0230
701-328-4114
Fax: 701-328-2961

OHIO
Ohio Board of Regents
P.O. Box 182452
Columbus, OH 43218-2452
888-833-1133
Fax: 614-752-5903

OKLAHOMA
Oklahoma State Regents for Higher
Education
500 Education Building
Oklahoma City, OK 73105-4503
405-858-4356
Fax: 405-858-4577

OREGON
Oregon State Scholarship Commission
1500 Valley River Drive, Suite 100
Eugene, OR 97401-2130
800-452-8807
Fax: 541-687-7419
www.ossc.state.or.us

PENNSYLVANIA
Pennsylvania Higher Education Assistance
    Authority
1200 North Seventh Street
Harrisburg, PA 17102-1444
800-692-7435
www.pheaa.org

RHODE ISLAND

Rhode Island Higher Education Assistance
Authority
560 Jefferson Boulevard
Warwick, RI 02886
401-736-1170
Fax: 401-736-3541
TDD: 401-222-6195

SOUTH CAROLINA

South Carolina Higher Education Tuition
Grants Commission
P.O. Box 12159
Columbia, SC 29211
803-734-1200
Fax: 803-734-1426
www.state.sc.us/tuitiongrants

SOUTH DAKOTA

Department of Education and Cultural
Affairs
Office of the Secretary
700 Governors Drive
Pierre, SD 57501-2291
605-773-3134
Fax: 605-773-6139

TENNESSEE

Tennessee Student Assistance Corporation
404 James Robertson Parkway, Suite 1950
Nashville, TN 37243
800-342-1663
615-741-1346
Fax: 615-741-6101
www.state.tn.us/tsac

TEXAS

Texas Higher Education Coordinating Board
P.O. Box 12788, Capitol Station
Austin, TX 78711
800-242-3062
Fax: 512-427-6420

UTAH

Utah State Board of Regents
Utah System of Higher Education
355 West North Temple
#3 Triad Center, Suite 550
Salt Lake City, UT 84180-1205
801-321-7200
Fax: 801-321-7299

VERMONT

Vermont Student Assistance Corporation
P.O. Box 2000
Winooski, VT 05404-2601
800-642-3177
800-655-9602
Fax: 800-654-3765
E-mail: info@vsac.org
www.vsac.org

VIRGINIA

State Council of Higher Education for Virginia
James Monroe Building
101 North Fourteenth Street
Richmond, VA 23219-3684
804-786-1690
Fax: 804-225-2604

WASHINGTON

Washington State Higher Education
Coordinating Board
P.O. Box 43430
917 Lakeridge Way
Olympia, WA 98501-3430
360-753-7850
Fax: 360-753-7808
E-mail: info@hecb.wa.gov
www.hecb.wa.gov

WEST VIRGINIA

State College & University Systems of West
Virginia Central Office
1018 Kanawha Boulevard East, Suite 700
Charleston, WV 25301-2827
304-558-4016
Fax: 304-558-0259

WISCONSIN

Higher Educational Aids Board
P.O. Box 7885
Madison, WI 53707-7885
608-267-2944
Fax: 608-267-2808
http://heab.state.wi.us

WYOMING

Wyoming Community College Commission
2020 Carey Avenue, 8th Floor
Cheyenne, WY 82002
307-777-7763
Fax: 307-777-6567

PROFESSIONAL ASSOCIATIONS

Accolade Network, Inc. (real estate appraiser network)
National Assignment Center
415 G Street
Modesto, CA 95351
209-522-9981
www.appraise.com

American Industrial Real Estate Association
700 South Flower Street, Suite 600
Los Angeles, CA 90017
213-687-8777
www.airea.com

The American Real Estate Society (ARES)
College of Business & Public Administration
Gamble Hall, Room 160A
University of North Dakota
P.O. Box 7120
Grand Forks, ND 58202-7120
701-777-3670
www.aresnet.org

American Society of Appraisers
555 Herndon Parkway Suite 125
Herndon, VA 20170
703-478-2228
www.appraisers.org

American Society of Asset Managers
303 West Cypress Street
P.O. Box 12528
San Antonio, TX 78212
800-486-3676
E-mail: czh@lincoln-grad.org

American Society of Farm Managers and
Rural Appraisers
950 South Cherry Street, Suite 508
Denver, CO 80246
303-758-3513
www.asfmra.org

American Society of Home Inspectors
932 Lee Street, Suite 101
Des Plaines IL 60016-6546
800-743-ASHI
www.ashi.com

Building Owners and Managers Association
International
1201 New York Avenue NW, Suite 300
Washington, D.C. 20005
202-408-2662
www.boma.org

Commercial Investment Real Estate Institute
430 North Michigan Avenue, 8th Floor
Chicago, IL 60611
800-621-7027
www.ccim.com

Community Associations Institute
225 Reinekers Lane, Suite 300
Alexandria, VA 22314
703-548-8600
www.caionline.org

Home Inspections-USA
Home Inspection Directory Corp.
P.O. Box 1465
North Hampton, NH 03862
877-491-2171
www.homeinspections-usa.com

Inman Real Estate News
1250 45th Street, Suite 360
Emeryville, CA 94608
510-658-9217
E-mail: info@inman.com
www.inman.com

Institute of Real Estate Management
430 North Michigan Avenue
Chicago, IL 60611-4090
312-329-6000
www.irem.org

International Real Estate Institute
1224 North Nokomis NE
Alexandria, MN 56308
320-763-4648
E-mail: irei@iami.org
www.iami.org/irei.cfm

Mortgage Bankers Association of America
1919 Pennsylvannia Avenue, NW
Washington, D.C. 20006-3438
202-557-2700
www.mbaa.org

NACORE International (formerly
   International Association of Corporate
   Real Estate Executives)
440 Columbia Drive, Suite 100
West Palm Beach, FL 33409
800-726-8111
www.nacore.com

National Apartment Association
201 North Union Street, Suite 200
Alexandria, VA 22314
703-518-6141
www.naahq.org

National Association of Real Estate
Appraisers
1224 North Nokomis, NE
Alexandria, MN 56308
320-763-7626
E-mail: narea@iami.org
www.iami.org/narea.cfm

National Association of Real Estate Brokers
1629 K Street, NW, Suite 1100
Washington, D.C. 20006
202-785-4477
E-mail: info@nareb.com
www.nareb.com

National Association of REALTORS®
700 11th Street, N.W.
Washington, D.C. 20001
202-383-1000
www.realtor.com

National Association of Residential Property
   Managers
P.O. Box 140647
Austin, TX 78714-0647
800-782-3452
E-mail: info@narpm.org
www.narpm.org

National Property Management Association
1108 Pinehurst Road, Oaktree Center
Dunedin, FL 34698
727-736-3788
www.npma.org

Real Estate Brokerage Managers Council
430 North Michigan Avenue
Chicago, IL 60611-4092
800-621-8738
www.crb.com

Real Estate Educators Association
320 West Sabal Palm Place, Suite 150
Longwood, FL 32779
407-834-6688
www.reea.org

Real Estate Law Institute
303 West Cypress Street
San Antonio, TX 78212
210-225-2897

The Real Estate Professional magazine
Wellesley Publications, Inc.
Needham, MA 02492
781-444-4688
www.therealestatepro.com

Realty Times
5949 Sherry Lane, Suite 1250
Dallas, TX 75225
214-353-6980
www.realtytimes.com

Society of Industrial and Office REALTORS®
700 11th Street NW, Suite 510
Washington, D.C. 20001-4511
202-737-1150
www.sior.com

Women's Council of REALTORS®
430 North Michigan Avenue
Chicago, IL 60611
312-329-8483
www.wcr.org

STATE APPRAISERS' LICENSING AGENCIES

ALABAMA
Alabama Real Estate Appraiser Board
P.O. Box 304355
Montgomery, AL 36130-4355
334-242-8747
Fax: 334-242-8749
www.agencies.state.al.us/reab/

ALASKA
Board of Certified Real Estate Appraisers
333 Willoughby Avenue
P.O. Box 110806
Juneau, AK 99811-0806
907-465-2542
Fax: 907-465-2974
www.dced.state.ak.us/occ/papr.htm/

ARIZONA
Arizona Board of Appraisal
1400 West Washington, Suite 360
Phoenix, AZ 85007
602-542-1539
Fax: 602-542-1598

ARKANSAS
Arkansas Appraiser Licensing & Certification
   Board
2725 Cantrell Road, Suite 202
Little Rock, AR 72202
501-296-1843
Fax: 501-296-1844

CALIFORNIA
Office of Real Estate Appraisers
1755 Creekside Oaks Drive #190
Sacramento, CA 95833
916-263-0722
Fax: 916-263-0887
www.orea.ca.gov/

COLORADO
State of Colorado Board of Real Estate
   Appraisers
1900 Grant Street, Suite 600
Denver, CO 80203
303-894-2166
Fax: 303-894-2683
www.dora.state.co.us/real-
estate/appraisr/appraisr.htm/

CONNECTICUT
Department of Consumer Protection
Real Estate Appraisal Division
State Office Building, Room G-8A
165 Capitol Avenue
Hartford, CT 06106
860-566-1568
Fax: 860-566-7630

DELAWARE
Delaware Council on Real Estate Appraisers
Professional Regulation Division
P.O. Box 1401
Cannon Building, Suite 203
Dover, DE 19903
302-739-4522
Fax: 302-739-6148

DISTRICT OF COLUMBIA
DCRA/OPLA
614 H. Street, NW, Room 921
Washington, D.C. 20013-7200
202-727-7450
Fax: 202-727-7662

FLORIDA
Florida Department of Business and
Professional Regulation
Division of Real Estate, Appraisal Section
400 West Robinson Street
Hurston North Tower
Orlando, FL 32801-1772
407-245-0800
Fax: 407-317-7254
www.state.fl.us/dbpr/re/index.shtml

GEORGIA
Georgia Real Estate Appraiser Board
International Tower
229 Peachtree Street, NE, Suite 1000
Atlanta, GA 30303-1605
404-656-3916
Fax: 404-656-0529
www.state.ga.us/Ga.Real_Estate/

HAWAII
Hawaii Real Estate Appraiser Program
1010 Richard Street
Honolulu, HI 96813
808-586-2693
Fax: 808-586-2689

IDAHO
Idaho Real Estate Appraiser Board
Bureau of Occupational Licenses
Owyhee Plaza
1109 Main Street, Suite 220
Boise, ID 83702-5642
208-334-3233
Fax: 208-334-3945
www.state.id.us/ibol/rea.htm

ILLINOIS
Illinois Real Estate Appraisal Administration
500 East Monroe Street, Suite 500
Springfield, IL 62701-1509
217-785-9638
Fax: 217-782-2549
www.obre.state.il.us/

INDIANA
Indiana Professional Licensing Agency
302 West Washington, Room EO34
Indianapolis, IN 46204-2700
317-232-7209
Fax: 317-232-2312

IOWA
Iowa Real Estate Appraiser Examining Board
1918 SE Hulsizer Avenue
Ankeny, IA 50021-3941
515-281-7363
Fax: 515-281-7411
www.state.ia.us/iapp

KANSAS
Kansas Real Estate Commission
820 South Quincy, Suite 314
Topeka, KS 66612
913-296-0706
Fax: 913-296-1934
www.ink.org/public/kreab/

KENTUCKY
Kentucky Real Estate Appraisers Board
3572 Iron Works Pike, Room 308
Lexington, KY 40511-8410
606-255-0144
Fax: 606-255-0661
E-mail: kreab@cjnetworks.com
www.kyappraisersboard.com

LOUISIANA
Louisiana Real Estate Commission
9071 Interline Avenue
P.O. Box 14785
Baton Rouge, LA 70898
504-925-4771
Fax: 504-925-4431

MAINE
Maine Board of Real Estate Appraisers
35 State House Station
122 Northern Avenue
Augusta, ME 04333
207-624-8603
Fax: 207-624-8637
www.maineprofessionalreg.org

MARYLAND

Maryland Department of Licensing &
Regulation
Real Estate Appraisers Commission
501 St. Paul Place, Room 902
Baltimore, MD 21202
410-333-4620
Fax: 410-333-6314
www.diir.state.md.us

MASSACHUSETTS

Commonwealth of Massachusetts
Division of Registration
100 Cambridge Street, Room 1512
Boston, MA 02202
617-727-3055
Fax: 617-727-2197
www.state.ma.us/reg/boards/re/default.htm/

MICHIGAN

Department of Consumer & Industry Service
Bureau of Occupational & Professional
Regulation
P.O. Box 30018
Lansing, MI 48909
517-335-1686
Fax: 517-373-2795

MINNESOTA

Minnesota Department of Commerce
133 East 7th Street
St. Paul, MN 55101
612-296-6319
Fax: 612-296-4328
www.commerce.state.mn.us/index.htm

MISSISSIPPI

Mississippi Real Estate Commission
5176 Keele Street
P.O. Box 12685
Jackson, MS 39236-2685
601-987-3969
Fax: 601-987-4173

MISSOURI

Missouri Real Estate Appraisers
Commission
P.O. Box 1335
Jefferson City, MO 65102
573-751-0038
Fax: 573-526-2831
www.ecoder.state.mo.us/pr/rea/default.htm

MONTANA

Board of Real Estate Appraisers
111 North Jackson
P.O. Box 200513
Helena, MT 59620-0513
406-444-3561
Fax: 406-444-1667
www.com.state.mt.us/LICENSE/pol/pol_
boards/rea_board/statutes.htm

NEBRASKA

Nebraska Real Estate Appraiser Board
301 Centennial Mall South
State Office Building, 3rd Floor
P.O. Box 9496
Lincoln, NE 68509-4963
402-471-9015
Fax: 402-471-9017
www.state.nv.us/b&i/red/

NEVADA

State of Nevada, Real Estate Division
Capitol Complex
1665 Hot Springs Road, Room 155
Carson City, NV 89710
702-687-6428
Fax: 702-687-4868

NEW HAMPSHIRE

New Hampshire Real Estate Appraiser
    Board
State House Annex, Room 426
25 Capitol Street
Concord, NH 03301-6312
603-271-6186
Fax: 603-271-6513

NEW JERSEY
Board of Real Estate Appraisers
Division of Consumer Affairs
124 Halsey Street
P.O. Box 45032
Newark, NJ 07101
201-504-6480
Fax: 201-648-3536
www.state.nj.us/lps/ca/nonmed.htm/

NEW MEXICO
New Mexico Real Estate Appraisers Board
1599 St. Francis Drive
P.O. Box 25101
Santa Fe, NM 87504
505-827-7554
Fax: 505-827-7560
www.rld.state.nm.us/

NEW YORK
Department of State
Division of Licensing Services
84 Holland Avenue
Albany, NY 12208-3490
518-473-2728
Fax: 518-473-2730
www.dos.state.ny.us/lcns/appraise.html

NORTH CAROLINA
North Carolina Appraisal Board
P.O. Box 20500
Raleigh, NC 27619-0500
919-420-7920
Fax: 919-420-7925

NORTH DAKOTA
North Dakota Appraisal Board
P.O. Box 1336
Bismarck, ND 58502-1336
701-222-1051
Fax: 701-222-8083

OHIO
Ohio Division of Real Estate
615 Superior Avenue, NW, Room 525
Cleveland, OH 44113
216-787-3100
Fax: 216-787-4449
www.com.state.oh.us

OKLAHOMA
Oklahoma Real Estate Appraisal Board
3814 North Santa Fe
P.O. Box 53408
Oklahoma City, OK 73152-3408
405-521-6636
Fax: 405-522-3642
www.oid.state.ok.us/agentbrokers/index.html

OREGON
Appraiser Certification and Licensure Board
Department of Consumer & Business
Services
350 Winter Street, NE, Room 21
Salem, OR 97310
503-373-1505
Fax: 503-378-6576

PENNSYLVANIA
Pennsylvania State Board of Certified Real
Estate Appraisers
124 Pine Street 1st Floor
Harrisburg, PA 17101
717-783-4866
Fax: 717-787-7769
www.dos.state.pa.us/bpoa/creabd/
licensureinfo.htm

RHODE ISLAND
Department of Business Regulation Licensing
Division of Commerce
Licensing & Regulation Real Estate
Appraisal Section
233 Richmond Street,
Providence, RI 02903
401-277-2262
Fax: 401-277-6654

SOUTH CAROLINA
South Carolina Real Estate Appraisal Board
3600 Forest Drive, Suite 100
P.O. Box 11329
Columbia, SC 29211-1329
803-734-4283
Fax: 803-734-4167
www.llr.state.sc.us/

SOUTH DAKOTA
South Dakota Department of Commerce and
Regulation
500 East Capitol
Pierre, SD 57501
605-773-3178
Fax: 605-773-3018
www.state.sd.us/state/executive/dcr/dcr.htm

TENNESSEE
Tennessee Real Estate Appraiser
Commission
500 James Robertson Parkway
2nd Floor
Nashville, TN 37243
615-741-1831
Fax: 615-741-6470
www.state.tn.us/commerce/regbrdiv.html

TEXAS
Texas Appraiser Licensing & Certification
Board
P.O. Box 12188
Austin, TX 78711-2188
512-465-3950
Fax: 512-465-3953
www.talcb.state.tx.us

UTAH
Utah Division of Real Estate
Department of Commerce
Box 146711
Salt Lake City, UT 84145
801-530-6747
Fax: 801-530-6749
www.commerce.state.ut.us/re/vdre1.htm

VERMONT
Secretary of States Office
Vermont Board of Real Estate Appraisers
P.O. Box 109 State Street
Montpelier, VT 05609-1106
802-828-3256
Fax: 802-828-2484
www.vtprofessionals.org/appraisers

VIRGINIA
Department of Professional & Occupational
Regulation
3600 West Broad Street, 5th Floor
Richmond, VA 23230-4817
804-367-2039
Fax: 804-367-2475
www.state.va.us/dpor/indexie.html

WASHINGTON
Business & Professions Division
P.O. Box 9015
Olympia, WA 98507-9015
360-753-1062
Fax: 360-586-0998
www.wa.gov/dol/bpd/appfront.htm

WEST VIRGINIA
West Virginia Real Estate Appraiser
Licensing and Certification Board
2110 Kanawha Boulevard, East, Suite 101
Charleston, WV 25311
304-558-3919
Fax: 304-558-3983
www.state.wv.us/appraise/

WISCONSIN
Wisconsin Department of Regulation &
Licensing
Business & Design Professions
P.O. Box 8935
Madison, WI 53708
608-266-1630
Fax: 608-267-3816
www.state.wi.us/agencies/drl/

WYOMING
Certified Real Estate Appraiser Board
First Bank Building
2020 Carey Avenue, Suite 100
Cheyenne, WY 82002-0180
307-777-7141
Fax: 307-777-3796
www.realestate.state.wy.us/

Appendix C

Directory of Real Estate Training Programs

THE SCHOOLS listed below are not endorsed or recommended by LearningExpress; they are intended to help you begin your search for an appropriate school by offering a representative listing of accredited or licensed schools in each state. Due to space limitations, all of the schools offering real estate education could not be listed here. The training offered by the institutions on the list range from a 45-hour course to a bachelor's degree and beyond. Therefore, you should contact each school to find out exactly what type of real estate training they offer.

For additional information on real estate training programs, see Chapter 3 for the names and contact information of state real estate licensing agencies. Most states have websites that include lists of approved schools; otherwise, call to request a list.

ALABAMA

Jefferson State Community College
2601 Carson Road
Birmingham, AL 35215
205-853-1200
www.jscc.cc.al.us

John C. Calhoun State Community College
P.O. Box 2216
Decatur, AL 35609-2216
256-306-2593
www.calhoun.cc.al.us

Enterprise State Junior College
P.O. Box 1300
Enterprise, AL 36331
334-393-ESJC
www.esjc.cc.al.us

Wallace State Community College
P.O. Box 2000
801 Main Street
Hanceville, AL 35077-2000
256-352-8000
www.wallacestatehanceville.edu

Alabama Institute of Real Estate
3938B Government Boulevard, Suite 101
Mobile, AL 36693
334-666-6765

Northeast Alabama State Community
  College
138 AL Highway 35 East
P.O. Box 159
Rainsville, AL 35986
256-228-6001
www.nacc.cc.al.us

University of Alabama
P.O. Box 870132
Tuscaloosa, AL 35487-0132
205-348-5666
www.ua.edu

ALASKA

Commonwealth School of Real Estate
4105 Turnagain Boulevard
Anchorage, AK 99517
907-248-1717
www.pacificrimproperties.com

University of Alaska
3211 Providence Drive
Anchorage AK 99508-8046
907-786-1800
www.uaa.alaska.edu

ARIZONA

Arizona Institute of Real Estate
2627 East 7th Avenue
Flagstaff, AZ 86004
520-526-6091
www.azinst.com

Glendale Community College
6000 West Olive Avenue
Glendale, AZ 85302
623-845-3000
www.gc.maricopa.edu

Mohave Community College
1971 Jagerson Avenue
Kingman, AZ 86401
520-757-0879
www.mohave.cc.az.us

Mesa Community College
1833 West Southern Avenue
Mesa, AZ 85202
480-461-7000
www.mc.maricopa.edu

Bud Crawley Real Estate School
5251 North 16th Street, Suite H-250
Phoenix, AZ 85016
602-263-0090

Paradise Valley Community College
18401 North 32nd Street
Phoenix, AZ 85032
602-787-6500
www.pvc.maricopa.edu

Phoenix College
1202 West Thomas Road
Phoenix, AZ 85013
602-264-2492
www.pc.maricopa.edu

Professional Institute of Real Estate
10207 North Scottsdale Road
Scottsdale, AZ 85253
480-991-0182
www.pire.com

Scottsdale Community College
9000 East Chaparral Road
Scottsdale, AZ 85250-2626
480-423-6100
www.sc.maricopa.edu

Arizona College of Real Estate
2876 Saint Andrews Drive
Sierra Vista, AZ 85635
520-378-6210

Arizona State University, Main Campus
Box 870112
Tempe, AZ 85287-0112
480-965-9011
www.asu.edu

Brodsky School of Real Estate
720 South Craycroft Road
Tucson, AZ 85711
520-747-1485

Hogan School of Real Estate
4023 East Grant Road
Tucson, AZ 85712
520-327-6849
-or-
800-794-1390
www.hoganschool.com

Pima Community College
4905 East Broadway Boulevard
Tucson, AZ 85709-1010
520-206-4500
www.pima.edu

ARKANSAS
ERA Collins School of Real Estate
10201 West Markham, Suite 306
Little Rock, AR 72205
501-224-2212

National Real Estate School
5323 John F. Kennedy Boulevard
North Little Rock, AR 72116
501-753-1633

Real Estate Education Center
3418 West Sunset, Suite E
P.O. Box 6686
Springdale, AR 72762
501-750-2772
www.propertystore.com

Arkansas State University
P.O. Box 1630
State University, AR 72467-1630
870-972-3024
-or-
800-382-3030
www.astate.edu

CALIFORNIA
Mercury Real Estate Schools
24490 Sunnymead Blvd.
Suite 102
Moreno Valley, CA 92553
714-778-3305
www.mercuryrealestatesch.com

Cabrillo College
6500 Soquel Drive
Aptos, CA 95003
831-479-6100
www.cabrillo.cc.ca.us

West Coast Schools
5385 El Camino Real
Atascadero, CA 93422
805-466-7843
www.westcoastschools.com

Bakersfield College
1801 Panorama Drive
Bakersfield, CA 93305
661-395-4011
www.bc.cc.ca.us

California State University, Dominguez Hills
1000 East Victoria Street
Carson, CA 90747
310-243-3645
www.csudh.edu

Southwestern College
900 Otay Lakes Road
Chula Vista, CA 91910
619-421-6700
www.swc.cc.ca.us

West Hills College at Coalinga
300 Cherry Lane
Coaling, CA 93210
559-935-0801
www.westhills.cc.ca.us

Compton Community College
1111 East Artesia Boulevard
Compton, CA 90221
310-900-1600
www.compton.cc.ca.us

West Los Angeles College
4800 Freshman Drive
Culver City, CA 90230
310-287-4200
www.wlac.cc.ca.us

DeAnza College
21250 Stevens Creek Boulevard
Cupertino, CA 95014
408-864-5678
www.deanza.fhda.edu

Cuyamaca College
900 Rancho San Diego Parkway
El Cajon, CA 92019
619-660-4000
http://cuyamaca.gcccd.cc.ca.us

Metropolitan Collegiate Institute
16661 Ventura Boulevard, Suite 518
Encino, CA 91436
818-990-3100

College of the Redwoods
7351 Tompkins Hill Road
Eureka, CA 95501-9300
707-476-4100

Coastline Community College
1146 Warner Avenue
Fountain Valley, CA 92708-2597
714-546-7600
www.cccd.edu

Ohlone College
43600 Mission Boulevard
Fremont, CA 94539-0390
510-659-6000
www.ohlone.cc.ca.us

California State University, Fresno
5241 North Maple Avenue
Fresno, CA 93740-8027
559-278-4240
www.csufresno.edu

Fresno City College
1101 East University Avenue
Fresno, CA 93741
559-442-4600
www.fcc.ca.us

Fullerton College
321 East Chapman Avenue
Fullerton, CA 92632-2095
714-992-7568
www.fullcoll.edu

Exacta Real Estate Schools
22691 Lambert Street, Suite 504
Lake Forest, CA 92630
949-462-0084 or 800-537-9061
www.nos.net/exacta

Rainbow Real Estate School
8342 Garden Grove Boulevard, Suite 6
Garden Grove, CA 92644
714-636-9340

Gavilan College
5055 Santa Teresa Boulevard
Gilroy, CA 95020
408-847-1400
www.gavilan.cc.ca.us

Glendale Community College
1500 North Verdugo Road
Glendale, CA 91208
818-240-1000
www.glendale.cc.ca.us

Citrus College
1000 West Foothill Boulevard
Glendora, CA 91741-1899
818-914-1899
www.citrus.cc.ca.us

Anthony Schools
2646 Dupont Drive
#230 2nd Floor
Irvine, CA 92612
818-368-4206
www.anthonyschools.com

California State University, Hayward
25800 Carlos Bee Boulevard
Hayward, CA 94542-3000
885-881-3817

Chabot College
25555 Hesperian Boulevard
Hayward, CA 94545
510-723-6600

Golden West College
15744 Golden West Street
P.O. Box 2748
Huntington Beach, CA 92647-2748
714-892-7711
www.gwc.cccd.edu

Imperial Valley College
380 East Aten Road
P.O. Box 158
Imperial, CA 92251
760-352-8320
www.imperial.cc.ca.us

College of Marin
835 College Avenue
Kentfield, CA 94904
415-457-8811
www.marin.cc.ca.us

Allied Real Estate Schools
22952 Alcalde Drive, Suite 150
Laguna Hills, CA 92653
800-542-5543
www.realestatelicense.com

Antelope Valley College
3041 West Avenue K
Lancaster, CA 93536
661-722-6300
www.avc.edu

California State University-Long Beach
1250 Bellflower Boulevard
Long Beach, CA 90840
562-985-4111
www.csulb.edu

Long Beach City College
4901 East Carson Street
Long Beach, CA 90808-1706
562-938-4205
www.lbcc.cc.ca.us

Foothill College
12345 El Monte Road
Los Altos Hills, CA 94022
650-949-7320
www.foothill.fhda.edu

California Association of REALTORS®
525 S. Virgil Avenue
Los Angeles, CA 90020
213-739-8200
www.car.org

California State University, Los Angeles
5151 State University Drive
Los Angeles, CA 90032-4226
323-343-3000
www.calstatela.edu

Los Angeles City College
855 North Vermont Avenue
Los Angeles, CA 90029
323-953-4000
http://citywww.lacc.cc.ca.us

Los Angeles Trade-Technical College
400 West Washington Boulevard
Los Angeles, CA 90015
213-744-9058
www.lattc.cc.ca.us

University of Southern California
University Park
Los Angeles, CA 90089-0911
213-740-6364

Merced College
3600 M Street
Merced, CA 95348
209-384-6187
www.merced.cc.ca.us

Saddleback College
28000 Marguerite Parkway
Mission Viejo, CA 92692-3635
949-582-4500
www.saddleback.cc.ca.us

Modesto Junior College
435 College Avenue
Modesto, CA 95350-5800
209-575-6470
http://mjc.yosemite.cc.ca.us

Monterey Peninsula College
980 Fremont Street
Monterey, CA 93940-4799
831-646-4000
www.mpc.edu

East Los Angeles College
1301 Cesar Chavez
Monterey Park, CA 91754
323-265-8650
www.elac.cc.ca.us

Napa Valley College
2277 Napa Vallejo Highway
Napa, CA 94558
707-253-3000
-or-
800-826-1077
www.nvc.cc.ca.us

California State University, Northridge
18111 Nordhoff Street
Northridge, CA 91330
818-677-1200
www.csun.edu

Cerritos College
11110 Alondra Blvd.
Norwalk, CA 90650-6298
562-860-2451
www3.cerritos.edu

Merritt College
12500 Campus Drive
Oakland, CA 94619
510-436-2444
www.merritt.edu

Mira Costa College
1 Barnard Drive
Oceanside, CA 92056
760-757-2121 or 1-888-201-8480
www.miracosta.cc.ca.us

Butte College
3536 Butte Campus Drive
Oroville, CA 95965-8303
530-895-2511
www.cin.butte.cc.ca.us

Oxnard College
4000 South Rose Avenue
Oxnard, CA 93033
805-986-5843
www.oxnard.cc.ca.us

College of the Desert
Desert Community College District
43500 Monterey Avenue
Palm Desert, CA 92260
760-346-8041
http:desert.cc.ca.us

California State Polytechnic University,
Pomona
3801 West Temple Avenue
Pamona, CA 91768
909-869-7659
www.csupomona.edu

Pasadena City College
1570 East Colorado Boulevard
Pasadena, CA 91106
626-585-7123
www.paccd.cc.ca.us

Los Medanos College
2700 East Leland Road
Pittsburg, CA 94565
925-439-2181
www.losmedanos.net

Diablo Valley College
321 Golf Club Road
Pleasant Hill, CA 94523-1544
925-685-1230
www.dvc.edu

Porterville College
100 East College Avenue
Porterville, CA 93257
559-791-2200
www.pc.cc.ca.us

Chaffey College
5885 Haven Avenue
Rancho Cucamonga, CA 91737-3002
909-987-1737
www.chaffey.cc.ca.us

Shasta College
P.O. Box 496006
Redding, CA 96049-6006
530-225-4769
www.shasta.cc.ca.us

Riverside Community College
4800 Magnolia Avenue
Riverside, CA 92506-1299
909-222-8000
www.rccd.cc.ca.us

Sierra College
Sierra Community College District
5000 Rocklin Road
Rocklin, CA 95677
916-624-3333
www.sierra.cc.ca.us

American River College
4700 College Oak Drive
Sacramento, CA 95841
916-484-8011
http://wserver.arc.losrios.cc.ca.us

California State University, Sacramento
6000 J Street
Sacramento, CA 95819
916-278-6011
www.csus.edu

Cosumnes River College
8401 Center Parkway
Sacramento, CA 95823-5799
916-691-7344
www.crc.losrios.cc.ca.us

Sacramento City College
3835 Freeport Boulevard
Sacramento, CA 95822-1386
916-558-2438
www.scc.losrios.cc.ca.us

Hartnell College
156 Homestead Avenue
Salinas, CA 93901
831-755-6700
www.hartnell.cc.ca.us

Realty Institute
2086 South E Street
San Bernadino, CA 92408
909-872-1933

San Bernadino Valley College
701 Mount Vernon Avenue
San Bernadino, CA 92410
909-888-6511
www.rccd.cc.ca.us

San Diego City College
1313 Twelfth Avenue
San Diego, CA 92101-4787
619-230-2470
www.city.sdccd.cc.ca.us

San Diego Mesa College
7250 Mesa College Drive
San Diego, CA 92111
619-388-2600
www.sdmesa.sdccd.cc.ca.us

San Diego State University
5500 Campanile Drive
San Diego, CA 92182
619-594-5200
www.sdsu.edu

City College of San Francisco
50 Phelan Avenue
San Francisco, CA 94112
415-239-3000
www.ccsf.cc.ca.us

San Francisco State University
1600 Holloway Avenue
San Francisco, CA 94132
415-338-2164
www.sfsu.edu

Mt. San Jacinto College
1499 North State Street
San Jacinto, CA 92583
909-487-6752
www.msjc.cc.ca.us

Evergreen Valley College
3095 Yerba Buena Road
San Jose, CA 95135
408-274-7900
www.evc.edu

San Jose City College
2100 Moorpark Avenue
San Jose, CA 95128
408-298-2181
www.sjcc.cc.ca.us

Cuesta College
P.O. Box 8106
San Luis Obispo, CA 93403
805-546-3100
www.cuesta.cc.ca.us

Palomar College
1140 West Mission Road
San Marcos, CA 92069-1487
760-744-1150
www.palomar.edu

College of San Mateo
1700 West Hillsdale Boulevard
San Mateo, CA 94402-3784
650-574-6161
http://gocsm.net

Contra Costa College
2600 Mission Bell Drive
San Pablo, CA 94806
510-235-7800
www.contracosta.cc.ca.us

Rancho Santiago College
1530 West 17th Street
Santa Ana, CA 92706-3398
714-564-6053

Santa Barbara City College
721 Cliff Drive
Santa Barbara, CA 93109
805-965-0581
www.sbcc.net

Mission College
3000 Mission College Boulevard
Santa Clara, CA 95054-1897
408-988-2200
www.wvmccd.cc.ca.us/mc/

Allan Hancock College
800 South College Drive
Santa Marias, CA 93454-6399
805-922-6966
www.hancock.cc.ca.us

Santa Rosa Junior College
1501 Mendocino Avenue
Santa Rosa, CA 95401-4395
707-527-4011 or 1-800-564-SRJC
www.santarosa.edu

West Valley College
14000 Fruitvale Avenue
Saratoga, CA 95070
408-867-2200
www.wvmccd.cc.ca.us/wvc/

Lake Tahoe Community College
One College Drive
South Lake Tahoe, CA 96150
530-541-4660
www.ltcc.cc.ca.us

San Joaquin Delta College
5151 Pacific Avenue
Stockton, CA 95207
209-954-5151
www.deltacollege.org

Solano County Community College District
4000 Suisun Valley Road
Suisun, CA 94585
707-864-7000
www.solano.cc.ca.us

Lassen Community College
P.O. Box 3000
Susanville, CA 96130
530-257-6181
www.lassen.cc.ca.us

Los Angeles Mission College
13356 Eldridge Avenue
Sylmar, CA 91342
818-364-7600
www.lamission.cc.ca.us

El Camino College
16007 Crenshaw Boulevard
Torrance, CA 90506
1-877-322-6466
www.elcamino.cc.ca.us

Mendocino College
1000 Hensley Creek Road
P.O. Box 3000
Ukiah, CA 95482
707-468-3102
www.mendocino.cc.ca.us

Ventura College
4667 Telegraph Road
Ventura, CA 93003
805-654-6400
www.ventura.cc.ca.us

Victor Valley Community College
18422 Bear Valley Road
Victorville, CA 92392-5849
760-245-4271
www.vvcconline.com

College of the Sequoias
915 South Mooney Boulevard
Visalia, CA 93277
559-730-3700
www.sequoias.cc.ca.us

San Joaquin Valley Institute
220 North Kolsey
Visalia, CA 93291-9283
559-651-2406
www.trainwithsjti.com

Mount San Antonio College
1100 North Grand Avenue
Walnut, CA 91789
909-594-5611
www.mtsac.edu

College of the Siskiyous
800 College Avenue
Weed, CA 96094
916-938-4461
www.siskiyous.edu

Rio Hondo College
3600 Workman Mill Road
Whittier, CA 90601
562-692-0921
www.rh.cc.ca.us

Los Angeles Harbor College
1111 Figueroa Place
Wilmington, CA 90744
310-522-8200
www.lahc.cc.ca.us

Los Angeles Pierce College
6201 Winnetka Avenue
Woodland Hills, CA 91371
818-347-0551
www.piercecollege.com

Los Angeles Valley College
5800 Fulton Avenue
Valley Glen, CA 91401
818-947-2600
www.lavc.cc.ca.us

Crafton Hills College
11711 Sand Canyon Road
Yucaipa, CA 92399
909-794-2161
www.sbccd.cc.ca.us/chc/

COLORADO

University of Colorado
Campus Box 178
Boulder, CO 80309
800-331-2801 or 303-492-1411
www.colorado.edu

Century 21 Academy Real Estate School
3520 Galley Road, Suite 200
Colorado Springs, CO 80909
719-574-9701
www.century21academy.com

Jones Real Estate College
1919 North Union Boulevard
Colorado Springs, CO 80909
719-473-0385
www.jonescollege.com

Pikes Peak Community College
5675 S. Academy Boulevard
Colorado Springs, CO 80906
800-456-6847
www.ppcc.cccoes.edu

Colorado Real Estate Institute
1780 South Bellaire Street, Suite 222
Denver, CO 80222-4307
303-744-1363
www.creiwrei.com

Metropolitan State College of Denver
P.O. Box 173362
Denver, CO 80217
303-556-2400
www.mscd.edu

University of Denver
2199 South University Boulevard
Denver, CO 80208
303-871-2000
www.du.edu

Colorado State University
Fort Collins, CO 80523-0015
970-491-1101
www.colostate.edu

Morgan Community College
17800 Road 20
Ft. Morgan, CO 80701
800-622-0216 or 970-542-3100
www.mcc.cccoes.edu

Colorado Mountain College
P.O. Box 10001
Glenwood Springs, CO 81602
970-945-8691
www.coloradomtn.edu

Colorado Association of Realtors Real
Estate School
309 Inverness Way South
Inglewood, CO 80112
303-790-7099
www.colorealtor.org

Jefferson County Association of Realtors
Education Training Center
950 Wadsworth Boulevard
Lakewood, CO 80215
303-233-7831
www.jcar.com

Red Rocks Community College
13300 West Sixth Avenue
Lakewood, CO 80228-1255
303-986-6160
www.rrcc.cccoes.edu

Arapahoe Community College
5900 South Santa Fe Drive
P.O. Box 9002
Littleton, CO 80160-9002
303-797-4222
www.arapahoe.edu

Northeastern Junior College
100 College Drive
Sterling, CO 80751
800-626-4637
http://nejc.cc.co.us

A. J. Educational Services, Inc.
2930 West 72nd Avenue
Westminster, CO 80030
www.realestateclasses.com
303-426-6443

CONNECTICUT

Connecticut Association of Realtors
111 Founders Plaza, Suite 1101
East Hartford, CT 06108
860-290-6601
www.ctrealtor.com

Manchester Community College
60 Bidwell Street
Manchester, CT 06040
860-647-6000
www.mcc.commnet.edu

University of Connecticut
2131 Hillside Road
Storrs, CT 06269
203-486-2000
www.uconn.edu

DISTRICT OF COLUMBIA

American University
440 Massachusetts Avenue Northwest
Washington, D.C. 20016
202-885-6000
www.american.edu

George Washington University
2121 Eye Street, North West
Washington, D.C. 20052
202-994-1000
www.gwu.edu

FLORIDA

South Florida Community College
600 West College Drive
Avon Park, FL 33825
863-453-6661
www.sfcc.cc.fl.us

Florida Atlantic University
777 Glades Road
P.O. Box 3091
Boca Raton, FL 33431-0991
561-297-3000
www.fau.edu

Brevard Community College
1519 Clearlake Road
Cocoa, FL 32922-6597
321-632-1111
www.brevard.cc.fl.us

University of Miami
Coral Gables, FL 33124
305-284-2211
www.miami.edu

Broward Community College
225 East Las Olas Boulevard
Ft. Lauderdale, FL 33301
954-761-7465
www.broward.cc.fl.us

University of Florida
West University Avenue and 13th Street
Gainesville, FL 32611
352-392-3261
www.ufl.edu

Florida Community College at Jacksonville
501 West State Street
Jacksonville, FL 32202
904-633-8100
www.fccj.org

University of North Florida
4567 St. Johns Bluff Road South
Jacksonville, FL 32224
904-620-1000
www.unf.edu

Okaloosa-Walton Community College
College Boulevard
Niceville, FL 32578
850-678-5111
www.owcc.cc.fl.us

Valencia Community College
P.O. Box 3028
Orlando, FL 32802-3028
407-299-5000
www.valencia.cc.fl.us

Gulf Coast Community College
5230 West Highway 98
Panama City, FL 32401-1058
850-769-1551
www.gc.cc.fl.us

Bob Hogue School of Real Estate
5531 Ninth Street North
St. Petersburg, FL 33703
813-526-5338
www.bobhogue-school.com

Florida State University
Tallahassee, FL 32306
850-644-2525
www.fsu.edu

GEORGIA
Barney Fletcher School
Atlanta Institute of Real Estate
3200 Professional Parkway
Galleria 75, Suite 275
Atlanta, GA 30339

Georgia State University
University Plaza
519 One Park Place South
Atlanta, GA 30303
404-651-2000
www.gsu.edu

Morehouse College
830 Westview Drive Southwest
Atlanta, GA 30314
404-681-2800
www.morehouse.edu

Georgia Institute of Real Estate
5784 Lake Forrest Drive
Atlanta, GA 30328
404-257-0354
www.learningrealestate.com

University of Georgia
Athens, GA 30602
706-542-2112
www.uga.edu

Augusta State University
2500 Walton Way
Augusta, GA 30904
706-737-1401
www.aug.edu

Meybohm Institute of Real Estate
2848 Washington Road
Augusta, GA 30909
706-736-3375
-or-
800-241-9726
www.meybohm-realtors.com

Middle Georgia College
1100 Second Street
Cochran, GA 31014
912-934-6221
www.mgd.peachnet.edu

HAWAII
Fahrni School of Real Estate
98-277 Kamehameha Highway
Aiea, HI 96701
808-486-8444

Hawaii Institute of Real Estate
Gentry Pacific Design Center
560 North Nimitz Highway, Suite 220
Honolulu, HI 96817
808-521-0071
www.pixi.com

University of Hawaii-Manoa
2444 Dole Street
Honolulu, HI 96822
808-956-8111
www.uhm.hawaii.edu

IDAHO

Idaho Association of REALTORS®
1450 West Bannock Street
Boise, ID 83702
208-342-3585 or 1-800-621-7553
www.idahorealtors.com

Idaho Real Estate Education Council
633 North Fourth Street
P.O. Box 83720
Boise, ID 83720-0077
208-334-3285
www.z.state.id.us/irec

Eastern Idaho Technical College
1600 South 25th East
Idaho Falls, ID 83404-5788
208-524-3000 or 1-800-662-0261
www.eitc.edu

Lewis-Clark State College
500 8th Avenue
Lewiston, ID 83501
208-799-5272
www.lesc.edu

University of Idaho
Moscow, ID 083844
1-88-88-UIDAHO
www.uidaho.edu

Idaho State University
921 South 8th
Pocatello, ID 83209
208-282-3277
www.isu.edu

College of Southern Idaho
315 Falls Avenue
P.O. Box 1238
Twin Falls, ID 83303-1238
208-733-9554
www.csi.cc.id.us

ILLINOIS

Illinois Academy of Real Estate
316 North Lake Street
Aurora, IL 60506
800-238-5404
www.ilacademy.com

Southwestern Illinois College
Belleville Campus
2500 Carlyle Road
Belleville, IL 62221-5899
618-235-2700 or 1-800-222-5131
www.southwestern.cc.il.us

Parkland College
2400 West Bradley Avenue
Champaign, IL 61821
217-351-2200 or 1-800-346-8089
www.parkland.cc.il.us

City Colleges of Chicago
Harold Washington College
30 East Lake Street
Chicago, IL 60601
312-553-5600
www.ccc.edu/hwashington/

City Colleges of Chicago
Kennedy-King College
6800 South Wentworth Avenue
Chicago, IL 60621
773-602-5000
www.ccc.edu/kennedyking/home.htm

City Colleges of Chicago
Olive-Harvey College
10001 South Woodlawn Avenue
Chicago, IL 60628
773-291-6100
www.ccc.edu/oliveharvey/

Realtors Real Estate School
200 North Michigan Avenue, #601
Chicago, IL 60611
312-803-4910
www.rres-online.com

Prairie State College
202 South Halsted Street
Chicago Heights, IL 60411
708-709-3500
www.prairie.cc.il.us

McHenry County College
8900 U.S. Highway 14
Crystal Lake, IL 60012-3700
815-455-8716
www.mchenry.cc.il.us

Danville Area Community College
2000 East Main Street
Danville, IL 61832
217-443-3222
-or-
888-455-3222
www.dacc.cc.il.us

Illinois Academy of Real Estate
Tom Brinkoetter Company
1698 East Pershing Road
Decatur, IL 62526
217-875-0555

Richland Community College
One College Park
Decatur, IL 62521
217-875-7200
www.richland.cc.il.us

Oakton Community College
1600 East Golf Road
Des Plaines, IL 60016
847-635-1703
www.oakton.edu

Sauk Valley Community College
173 Illinois Route 2
Dixon, IL 61021
815-288-5511
www.svcc.cc.il.us

Illinois Central College
One College Drive
East Peoria, IL 61635-0001
309-694-5011
www.icc.cc.il.us

Elgin Community College
1700 Spartan Drive
Elgin, IL 60123
847-697-1000
http://elgin.cc.il.us

Northwestern University
633 Clark Street
Evanston, IL 60208
847-491-3741
www.northwestern.edu

Carl Sandburg College
2400 Tom L. Wilson Boulevard
Galesburg, IL 61401
309-344-2518
www.csc.cc.il.us

College of DuPage
425 22nd Street
Glen Ellyn, IL 60137-6599
630-942-2482
www.cod.edu

Illinois Association of Realtors
P.O. Box 19451
Springfield, IL 62794-9451
217-529-2600
www.illinoisrealtor.org

Lewis and Clark Community College
5800 Godfrey Road
Godfrey, IL 62035-2466
618-467-2270 or 800-500-LCCC
www.lc.cc.il.us

College of Lake Country
19351 West Washington Street
Grayslake, IL 60030-1198
847-223-6601
www.clc.cc.il.us

Southeastern Illinois College
3575 College Road
Harrisburg, IL 62946-4925
618-252-5400
-or-
866-338-2742
www.sic.cc.il.us

Zittel School of Real Estate
4950 North Harlem Avenue
Harwood Heights, IL 60656
708-867-5757

Joliet Junior College
1215 Houbolt Road
Joliet, IL 60431-8938
815-729-9020
www.jjc.cc.il.us

Kankakee Community College
P.O. Box 888
Kankakee, IL 60901
815-933-0345
www.kcc.cc.il.us

Kishwaukee College
21193 Malta Road
Malta, IL 60150-9699
815-825-2086
http://kish.cc.il.us

Black Hawk College, Moline
6600 34th Avenue
Moline, IL 61265
309-796-1311
-or-
800-334-1311
www.bhc.edu

J-Mars School of Real Estate Education
4363 North Harlem Avenue
Norridge, IL 60634
708-457-2000

Coldwell Banker Institute of Real Estate
1211 West 22nd Street, Suite 700
Oakbrook, IL 60523
847-788-7943

Dabbs Academy of Real Estate
15567 South 94th Avenue
Oakland Park, IL 60462
708-535-5540

William Rainey Harper College
1200 West Algonquin Road
Palatine, IL 60067-7398
847-925-6000
www.harper.cc.il.us

Triton College
2000 Fifth Avenue
River Grove, IL 60171
708-456-0300
www.tritoncc.il.us

Rock Valley College
3301 North Mulford Road
Rockford, IL 61114-5699
815-654-4250
www.rvc.cc.il.us

South Suburban College
15800 South State Street
South Holland, IL 60473-1270
708-596-2000
www.ssc.cc.il.us

Lincoln Land Community College
5250 Shepard Road
P.O. Box 19256
Springfield, IL 62794-9256
217-786-2200 or 1-800-727-4161
www.llcc.cc.il.us

Waubonsee Community College
Route 47 at Waubonsee Drive
Sugar Grove, IL 60554-9454
630-466-7900
www.wcc.cc.il.us

Illinois University of Urbana-Champaign
506 South Wright Street
Urbana, IL 61801
217-333-0302
www.uiuc.edu

INDIANA

Indiana University-Bloomington
107 S. Indiana Avenue
Bloomington, IN 47405-7000
812-855-4848
www.iub.edu

Ivy Technical State College-Northeast
3800 North Anthony Boulevard
Fort Wayne, IN 46805
219-482-9171
www.ivy.tec.in.us

Indiana University - Purdue University
Indianapolis
425 University Boulevard
Indianapolis, IN 46202-5143
317-274-4591
www.iupui.edu

Vincennes University
Jasper Campus
850 College Avenue
Jasper, IN 47546
812-482-3030
www.vinu.edu

Ball State University
2000 University Avenue
Muncie, IN 47306
1-800-482-4278
www.bsu.edu

IOWA

Iowa Real Estate School of Cedar Rapids
385 Collins Road, Northeast
Cedar Rapids, IA 52402
319-393-4900
www.iowarealty.com/cedarrapids

Key Real Estate School
501 South Main
Council Bluffs, IA 51503
712-328-3133
www.keyre.com

Iowa Lakes Community College
300 South 18th Street
Estherville, IA 51334-2725
712-362-2604
-or-
800-521-5054
www.ilcc.cc.ia.us

Western Iowa Technical Community College
4647 Stone Avenue
P.O. Box 5199
Sioux City, IA 51102-5199
712-274-6400
www.witcc.com

Coldwell Banker Mid-America
Group of Real Estate
4800 Westown Parkway Suite 110
West Des Moines, IA 50266
515-224-8787

KANSAS

Dodge City Community College
2501 North Fourteenth Avenue
Dodge City, KS 67801-2399
316-225-1321
-or-
800-FOR-DCCC
www.dccc.cc.les.us

Butler County Community College
901 South Haverhill Road
El Dorado, KS 67042-3280
316-321-2222
www.buccc.cc.ks.us

Independence Community College
Brookside Drive and College Avenue
P.O. Box 708
Independence, KS 67301-0708
316-331-4100 or 800-842-6063
www.indy.cc.ks.us

Real Estate School of Kansas City
5210 Northeast Chouteau Trafficway
Kansas City, KS 64119-2509
816-453-3826
www.realestateprepschool.com

Haskell Indian Nations University
155 Indian Avenue, #5031
Lawrence, KS 66046-4800
785-749-8454
www.haskell.edu

Real Estate School of Lawrence
P.O. Box 3271
Lawrence, KS 66046

Topeka Institute of Real Estate
5120 West 28th
Topeka, KS 66614-2399
913-273-1330

Wichita State University
1845 Fairmount
Wichita, KS 67260
316-978-3045
www.wichita.edu

KENTUCKY

Ashland Community College
1400 College Drive
Ashland, KY 41101
800-370-7191
www.ashlandcc.org

Elizabethtown Community College
600 College Street Road
Elizabethtown, KY 42701
270-769-2371 or 877-2GO-2ECC
www.elizabethtowncc.com

University of Kentucky
Lexington Community College
Cooper Drive
Lexington, KY 40506
859-257-4872
www.uky.edu/lcc/

Realtors Institute
161 Prosperous Place
Lexington, KY 40509
859-263-7377
www.kar.com

Family Style School of Professional
Licensing
7711 Beulah Church Road
Louisville, KY 40228
502-231-2927

Madisonville Community College
2000 College Drive
Madisonville, KY 42431
270-821-2250
www.madcc.kctcs.net

Paducah Community College
4810 Alben Barkley Drive
P.O. Box 7380
Paducah, KY 42002-7380
270-554-9200
www.pccky.com

Prestonburg Community College
One Bert T. Combs Drive
Prestonburg, KY 41653-9502
606-886-3863

Eastern Kentucky University
521 Lancaster Avenue
Richmond, KY 40475
859-622-1000
www.eku.edu

LOUISIANA

Louisiana State University
Office of Undergraduate Admissions
110 Thomas Boyd Hall
Baton Rouge, LA 70803
225-578-1175
www.lsu.edu

Louisiana Technical College
Sullivan Campus
1710 Sullivan Drive
Bogalusa, LA 70427
504-732-6640 or 1-800-732-6640
www.sullivan.tec.la.us

Louisiana Technical College
Jefferson Campus
5200 Blair Drive
Metairie, LA 70001
504-736-7072
www.jeff.tec.la.us

University of Louisiana at Monroe
700 University Avenue
Monroe, LA 71209
318-342-5252 or 362-4661
www.ulm.edu

University of New Orleans
Lakefront
New Orleans, LA 70148
504-286-6000
www.uno.edu

Baker's Professional Real Estate College
1612 Fairfield Avenue
Shreveport, LA 71101
318-222-7459
www.bprec.com

Louisiana Technical College
Shreveport Bossier Campus
P.O. Box 78527
2010 North Market
Shreveport, LA 71107
318-676-7811

MAINE
University of Southern Maine
37 College Avenue
Gorham, ME 04038
800-800-4876 or 207-780-4141
www.usm.maine.edu

Thomas College
180 West River Road
Waterville, ME 04901-5097
207-859-1111
www.thomas.edu

MARYLAND
Champion Institute of Real Estate
541 Baltimore Annapolis Boulevard
Saverna Park, MD 21146
410-544-6004
www.championrealty.com

Anne Arundel Community College
101 College Parkway
Arnold, MD 21012
410-647-7100
www.aacc.cc.md.us

Harford Community College
401 Thomas Run Road
Bel Air, MD 21015
410-836-4000
www.harford.cc.md.us

Weichert Real Estate School
6610 Rockledge Drive, Suite 100
Bethesda, MD 20817
301-718-4143

Catonsville Community College
800 South Rolling Road
Catonsville, MD 21228
410-455-6050
www.ccbc.cc.md.us

O'Brien Institute of Real Estate
21780 Great Mills Road
Lexington Park, MD 20653
301-863-2991

Long & Foster Institute of Real Estate
200 Orchard Ridge Drive
Gaithersburg, MD 20878
301-417-7100
www.longandfoster.com

Maryland School of Real Estate
7 Park Avenue
Gaithersburg, MD 20877
301-948-7200
www.re7.com/md/rred

Century 21 Real Estate School
160 Ritchie Highway #A2
Severna Park, MD 21146
410-766-5850

Diplomat Real Estate Center
5505 Sargent Road
Hyattsville, MD 20782
301-559-6000
www.realtor.com.washingtondc/
    diplomatrealty2000

Champion Institute of Real Estate
541B Baltimore-Annapolis Boulevard
Severna Park, MD 21146
410-544-6004
-or-
800-922-4794

Champion Institute of Real Estate
411 Thompson Creek
Stevensville, MD 21619
410-643-7454
www.championrealty.com

Villa Julie College
1525 Green Spring Valley Road
Stevenson, MD 21153-0641
410-486-7000
-or-
877-GO-TO-VJC
www.vjc.edu

Montgomery College
Takoma Park Campus
7600 Takoma Avenue
Takoma Park, MD 20912
301-650-1501
www.mc.cc.md.us

O'Conor, Piper & Flynn School of
    Real Estate
22 West Padonia Road
Timonium, MD 21093
410-261-8800
www.opf.com

Farrall Institute
Route 5 and Saint Charles Parkway
P.O. Box 40
Waldorf, MD 20604
301-645-1700
www.hungerfordassociates.com

MASSACHUSETTS

Northeastern University
360 Huntington Avenue
Boston, MA 02115
617-373-2000
www.northeastern.edu

Massachusetts Institute of Technology
Center for Real Estate
77 Massachusetts Avenue
Cambridge, MA 02139-4307
617-253-1000
http://web.mit.edu

Nichols College
Center Road
P.O. Box 5000
Dudley, MA 01571
800-470-3379
www.nichols.edu

Greenfield Community College
1 College Drive
Greenfield, MA 01301-9739
413-775-1801

Northern Essex Community College
100 Elliot Way
Haverhill, MA 01830
978-556-3600
www.necc.mass.edu

Greater Springfield Association of Realtors
School
221 Industry Avenue
P.O. Box 4826
Springfield, MA 01104
413-785-1328
www.greaterspringfieldassociationof
    realtors.com

MICHIGAN

Ferris State University
901 South State Street
Big Rapids, MI 49307
213-591-2000
www.ferris.edu

Henry Ford Community College
5101 Evergreen Road
Dearborn, MI 48128
313-845-9600 or 800-585-4322
www.henryford.cc.mi.us

Wayne County Community College
801 West Fort Street
Detroit, MI 48226
313-496-2600
www.wccc.edu

Kalamazoo Valley Community College-Texas
Township
6767 West "O" Avenue
P.O. Box 4070
Kalamazoo, MI 49003-4070
616-372-5000
www.kvcc.edu

Western Michigan University
1903 West Michigan Avenue
Kalamazoo, MI 49008-5201
616-387-1000
www.wmich.edu

Lansing Community College
419 North Capitol Avenue
P.O. Box 40010
Lansing, MI 48901-7210
517-483-1957 or 1-800-644-4LCC
www.lansing.cc.mi.us

Kirtland Community College
10775 North St. Helen Road
Roscommon, MI 48653
517-275-5000
www.kirtland.cc.mi.us

Delta College
University Center, MI 48710
517-686-9000
www.delta.edu

MINNESOTA

Itasca Community College
1851 East Highway 169
Grand Rapids, MN 55744-3397
218-327-4464
-or-
800-9966-ICC
www.it.cc.mn.us

Rainy River Community College
1501 Highway 71
International Falls, MN 56649
218-285-7722
www.rrcc.mnscu.edu

Mankato State University
MSU 55
Mankato, MN 56002-8400
507-389-1822
www.mankato.msus.edu

St. Cloud State University
720 Fourth Avenue South
St. Cloud, MN 56301-4498
320-255-0121
www.stcloudstate.edu

Ridgewater College
Willmar Campus
2101 15th Avenue NW
P.O. Box 1097
Wilmar, MN 56201
320-231-5114 or 800-722-1151
www.ridgewater.mnscu.edu

MISSISSIPPI

Delta State University
Cleveland, MS 38733
662-846-4655
www.deltast.edu

University of Southern Mississippi
2701 Hardy Street
Hattiesburg, MS 39406
601-266-5000
www.usm.edu

Mississippi State University
P.O. Box 5325
Mississippi State, MS 39762
662-325-2323
www.msstate.edu

Hinds Community College
P.O. Box 1100
Raymond, MS 39154-1100
601-857-3212
www.hinds.cc.ms.us

East Mississippi Community College
Scooba Campus
P.O. Box 158
Scooba, MS 39358
662-476-5041
www.emcc.cc.ms.us

Northwest Mississippi Community College
4975 Highway 51 North
Senatobia, MS 38668
662-562-3200
www.nwcc.cc.ms.us

University of Mississippi
Office of Admissions
145 Martindale
University, MS 38677
662-915-7226
www.olemiss.edu

MISSOURI
University of Missouri, Columbia
230 Jesse Hall
Columbia, MO 65211
573-882-7786
www.missouri.edu

St. Louis Community College
113333 Big Bend Boulevard
Kirkwood, MO 63122
314-984-7608
www.stlcc.cc.mo.us

Lindenwood College
209 South Kingshighway
St. Charles, MO 63301
636-949-4949
www.lindenwood.edu

St. Louis Community College at Florissant
Valley
3400 Pershall Road
St. Louis, MO 63135
314-595-4250
www.stl.cc.mo.us

Webster University
470 East Lockwood Boulevard
St. Louis, MO 63119
314-968-6900
www.webster.edu

Drury College
900 North Benton
Springfield, MO 65802
800-922-2274
www.drury.edu

Real Estate School of Springfield
306 East Pershing Street
Springfield, MO 65806
417-862-6677

Southwest Missouri State University
901 South National Avenue
Springfield, MO 65804
417-836-5000
www.smsu.edu

MONTANA
Connole-Morton Schools
415 North Higgins Avenue
Suite 20
Missoula, MT 59802
406-543-3269 or 1-800-845-7491
www.connole-morton.com

NEBRASKA

University of Nebraska at Kearney
905 West 25th Street
Kearney, NE 68849
308-865-8441
-or-
800-KEARNEY
www.unk.edu

Larabee School
225 North Cotner Boulevard #106
Lincoln, NE 68505
402-436-3308 or 800-755-1108
www.larabeeschool.com

Northeast Community College
801 East Benjamin Avenue
P.O. Box 469
Norfolk, NE 68702-0469
402-371-2020
http://alpha.necc.cc.ne.us

Mid-Plains Community College
1101 Halligan Drive
North Platte, NE 69101
308-532-8740
www.mpcca.cc.ne.us

Metropolitan Community College
P.O. Box 3777
Omaha, NE 68103-0777
402-457-2400 or 800-228-9553
www.mccneb.edu

Randall School of Real Estate
11224 Elm Street
Omaha, NE 68144
402-333-3004

University of Nebraska-Omaha
6001 Dodge Street
Omaha, NE 68182
402-554-2800
www.unomaha.edu

Western Nebraska Community College
1601 East 27th Street
Scottsbluff, NE 69361
308-635-6000
-or-
800-348-4435
www.wncc.net

NEVADA

Western Nevada Community College
2201 West College Parkway
Carson City, NV 89703
775-445-3000

Americana School of Real Estate
3790 Paradise Road, Suite 200
Las Vegas, NV 89109
702-796-8888
www.gettherock.com

Real Estate School of Nevada
4180 South Sandhill Road, Unit B-10
Las Vegas, NV 89121
702-454-1936
www.realtyschool.com

Southern Nevada School of Real Estate
3441 West Sahara Avenue, Suite C1
Las Vegas, NV 89102-6059
702-364-2525 or 800-346-2520
www.snsore.com

University of Nevada, Las Vegas
4505 Maryland Parkway
Las Vegas, NV 89154
702-895-3011
www.unlv.edu

Community College of Southern Nevada
3200 East Cheyenne
North Las Vegas, NV 89030-4296
702-651-4060
www.ccsn.nevada.edu

Northern Nevada Real Estate School
3951 South McCarren Boulevard
Reno, NV 89502
775-829-1055

Truckee Meadows Community College
7000 Dandini Boulevard
Reno, NV 89512
775-673-7000
www.tmcc.edu

NEW HAMPSHIRE
New Hampshire Technical Institute
11 Institute Drive
Concord, NH 03301-7412
603-271-7134 or 800-247-0179
www.conc.tec.nh.us

NEW JERSEY
Camden County College
P.O. Box 200
College Drive
Blackwood, NJ 08012
856-227-7200
www.camdencc.edu

Century 21 West Division
6 Sylvan Way
Parsippany, NJ 07054
www.century21.com

Professional School of Business
22 East Willow Street
Millburn, NJ 07041
973-564-8686
www.proschool.com

Weichert Real Estate School
1625 Route 10 East
Morris Plains, NJ 07950
800-544-3000
www.schoolsofrealestate.com

Kovat's Real Estate and Insurance School
230 W. Passaic Street
Maywood, NJ 07607
201-843-7277

Burlington County College
County Route 530
Pemberton, NJ 08068
609-894-4900
www.bcc.edu

Princeton School of Real Estate
238 West Delaware Avenue
Pennington, NJ 08534
609-737-1525

Fairleigh Dickenson University
1000 River Road
Teaneck, NJ 07666
201-692-2000
www.fdu.edu

Gloucester County College
1400 Tanyard Road
Sewell, NJ 08080
856-468-5000
www.gccnj.edu

Raritan Valley Community College
P.O. Box 3300
Somerville, NJ 08876
908-526-1200
www.raritanval.edu

Ocean County College
College Drive
P.O. Box 2001
Toms River, NJ 08754-2001
732-255-0400
www.ocean.cc.nj.us

Thomas Edison State College
101 West State Street
Trenton, NJ 08608-1176
609-984-1150 or 1-800-882-8372
www.tesc.edu

South Jersey Professional School of
  Business
2121 Villa Shopping & Professional Center
Route 73
West Berlin, NJ 08091
609-767-0600

NEW MEXICO
New Mexico Real Estate Institute
8205 Spain Road Northeast, Suite 109
Albuquerque, NM 87109
505-821-5556

New Mexico State University-Alamogordo
2400 North Scenic Drive
Alamogordo, NM 88310
505-439-3600
http://alamo.nmsu.edu

Clovis Community College
417 Schepps Boulevard
Clovis, NM 88101-8381
505-769-2811
www.clovis.cc.nm.us

San Juan College
4601 College Boulevard
Farmington, NM 87401
505-326-3311
www.sjc.cc.nm.us

New Mexico Junior College
5317 Levington Highway
Hobbs, NM 88240
505-392-5092
www.nmjc.cc.nm.us

New Mexico State University
Box 30001 Dept. 3A
Las Cruces, NM 88003-8001
505-646-0111
www.nmsu.edu

University of New Mexico-Valencia Campus
280 La Entrada
Los Lunas, NM 87031
505-925-8500
www.unm.edu/~unmvc/

Eastern New Mexico University
Portales, NM 88130
800-367-3668
www.enmn.edu

Sante Fe Community College
6401 Richards Avenue
Santa Fe, NM 87505-4887
505-428-1270
www.santa-fe.cc.nm.us

NEW YORK

State University of New York
Alfred State College
College of Technology at Alfred
Alfred, NY 14802
1-800-4-ALFRED
www.suny.edu or www.alfredtech.edu

Queensborough Community College of the
   City University of New York
222-05 56th Avenue
Bayside, NY 11364
718-631-6262
www.qcc.cuny.edu

New York Real Estate Institute
347 Fifth Avenue 600A
New York, NY 10016
212-683-5518
www.nyrei.com

City University of New York-Lehman College
250 Bedford Park Boulevard West
Bronx, NY 10468-1589
718-960-8706 or 1-877-LEHMAN-1
www.lehman.cuny.edu

College of Technology at Canton
SUNY Canton
Cornell Drive
Canton, NY 13617
1-800-388-7123
www.canton.edu

Five Towns College
305 North Service Road
Dix Hills, NY 11746-5871
631-424-7000
www.fivetowns.edu

Nassau Community College
One Education Drive
Garden City, NY 11530
516-572-7345
www.sunynassau.edu

Columbia-Greene Community College
Box 1000
Hudson, NY 12534-0327
518-828-4181
www.sunycgcc.edu

Cornell University
Field of Real Estate
Ithaca, NY 14853
607-254-4636
www.cornell.edu

Orange County Community College
115 South Street
Middletown, NY 10940
845-344-6222
http://orange.cc.ny.us

Borough of Manhattan Community College
199 Chambers Street
New York, NY 10007
212-346-8000
www.bmcc.cuny.edu

New York University
70 Washington Square North
New York, NY 10012
212-998-1212
www.nyu.edu

Suffolk County Community College-Eastern
 Campus
121 Speonk-Riverhead Road
Riverhead, NY 11901
631-548-2564
www.sunysuffolk.edu/web/eastcampus

Suffolk County Community College-
Ammerman Campus
533 College Road
Seldon, NY 11784
631-451-4022
www.sunysuffolk.edu

Rockland Community College
145 College Road
Suffern, NY 10901
845-574-4000
www.sunyrockland.edu

Mohawk Valley Community College
1101 Sherman Drive
Utica, NY 13501
315-792-5400
www.mvcc.edu

Westchester Community College
75 Grasslands Road
Valhalla, NY 10595
914-785-6600
www.sunywcc.edu

NORTH CAROLINA
Stanley Community College
141 College Drive
Albemarle, NC 28001
704-982-0121
www.stanly.cc.nc.us

Randolph Community College
Asheboro Campus
P.O. Box 1009
Asheboro, NC 27204-1009
336-633-0200
www.randolph.cc.nc.us/randolph/

Appalachian State University
Boone, NC 28608
828-262-2000
www.appstate.edu

Central Piedmont Community College
P.O. Box 35009
Charlotte, NC 28235
704-330-2722
www.cpcc.cc.nc.us

Sampson Community College
P.O. Box 318
Highway 24 West
Clinton, NC 28329-0318
910-592-8081
www.sampson.cc.nc.us

Haywood Community College
185 Freedlander Drive
Clyde, NC 28721
828-627-2821
http://w3.haywood.cc.nc.us

Surry Community College
630 South Main Street
P.O. Box 304
Dobson, NC 27017
336-386-8121
www.surry.cc.nc.us

Bladen Community College
7418 NC Highway 41 West
P.O. Box 266
Dublin, NC 28332
910-862-2164
www.bcc.cc.nc.us

College of the Albermarle
1208 North Road Street
P.O. Box 2327
Elizabeth City, NC 27906-2327
252-335-0821
www.albemarle.cc.nc.us

Fayetteville Technical Community College
2201 Hull Road
Fayetteville, NC 28303
910-678-8204
www.faytech.cc.nc.us

Wayne Community College
3000 Wayne Memorial Drive
Goldsboro, NC 27534
919-735-5151
www.wayne.cc.nc.us

Alamance Community College
1247 Jimmie Kerr Road
P.O. Box 8000
Graham, NC 27253-8000
336-578-2002
www.almance.cc.nc.us

East Carolina University
East Fifth Street
Greenville, NC 27858-4353
252-328-6131
www.ecu.edu

Pitt Community College
P.O. Drawer 7007
Greenville, NC 27835-7007
252-321-4200
www.pitt.cc.nc.us

Catawba Valley Community College
Hickory, NC 28602-9699
704-327-7009
www.cvcc.cc.nc.us

Caldwell Community College and Technical
Institute
2855 Hickory Boulevard
Hudson, NC 28638-2397
828-726-2200
www.caldwell.cc.nc.us

Guilford Technical Community College
P.O. Box 309
Jamestown, NC 27282
336-334-4822
http://technet.gtcc.cc.nc.us

Davidson County Community College
P.O. Box 1287
Lexington, NC 27293-1287
336-751-2885
www.davidson.cc.nc.us

Carteret Community College
3505 Arendell Street
Morehead City, NC 28557
252-222-6000
http://gofish.carteret.cc.nc.us

Western Piedmont Community College
1001 Burkemont Avenue
Morgantown, NC 28655-4511
704-438-6000
www.wp.cc.nc.us

Tri-County Community College
4600 Highway 64 East
Murphy, NC 28906
828-837-6810
www.tccc.cc.nc.us

Craven Community College
800 College Court
New Bern, NC 28562
252-638-4131
www.craven.cc.nc.us

Sandhills Community College
2200 Airport Road
Pinehurst, NC 28374
910-692-6185 or 1-800-338-3944
www.sandhills.cc.nc.us

Wake Technical Community College
9101 Fayetteville Road
Raleigh, NC 27603
919-662-3500
www.wake.tec.nc.us

Central Carolina Community College
1105 Kelley Drive
Sanford, NC 27330
919-775-5401
www.ccarolina.cc.nc.us

Isothermal Community College
P.O. Box 804
Spindale, NC 28160
828-286-3636
www.isothermal.cc.nc.us

Mayland Community College
P.O. Box 547
200 Mayland Drive
Spruce Pine, NC 28777
828-765-7351
-or-
800-4-MAYLAND
www.mayland.cc.nc.us

Brunswick Community College
P.O. Box 30
Supply, NC 28462-0030
910-754-6900
www.brunswick.cc.nc.us

Southwestern Community College
Jackson/Sylva Campus
447 College Drive
Sylva, NC 28779
828-586-4091 or 1-800-447-4091
www.southwest.cc.nc.us

Edgecombe Community College
Tarboro, NC 27886-9399
252-823-5166
www.edgecombe.cc.nc.us

Beaufort County Community College
Highway 264 East
P.O. Box 1069
Washington, NC 27889
252-946-6194
www.beaufort.cc.nc.us

Rockingham Community College
P.O. Box 38
Wentworth, NC 27375
910-342-4261
www.rcc.cc.nc.us

Cape Fear Community College
411 North Front Street
Wilmington, NC 28401-3393
910-251-5100
http://cfcc.net

Forsyth Technical Community College
2100 Silas Creek Parkway
Winston-Salem, NC 27103
336-723-0371
www.forsyth.tec.nc.us

NORTH DAKOTA
Bismarck State College
P.O. Box 5587
1500 Edwards Avenue
Bismarck, ND 58506
800-445-5073
www.bsc.nodak.edu

North Dakota State College of Science
800 North Sixth Street
Wahpeton, ND 58076-0002
800-342-4325

OHIO

Southern Ohio College-Northeast Campus
2791 Mogadore
Akron, OH 44312-1596
330-733-8766

Northwest State Community College
22-600 State Route 34
Archbold, OH 43502
419-267-5511
www.nscc.cc.oh.us

Kent State University, Ashtabula Campus
3325 West 13th Street
Ashtabula, OH 44004
440-964-3322
www.ashtabula.kent.edu

University of Cincinnati-Clermont College
4200 Clermont College Drive
Batavia, OH 45103
513-732-5200
www.clc.uc.edu

Malone College
515 25th Street Northwest
Canton, OH 44709
330-471-8100
www.malone.edu

Cincinnati State Technical & Community
College
3520 Central Parkway
Cincinnati, OH 45223
513-569-1500
www.cinstate.cc.oh.us

University of Cincinnati-Access Colleges
100 Edwards Center
Cincinnati, OH 45221-0091
513-556-1100
www.uc.edu

University of Cincinnati-Raymond Walters
College
9555 Plainfield Road
Cincinnati, OH 45236-1096
513-745-5700
www.rwc.uc.edu

Cuyahoga Community College-Metropolitan
Campus
2900 Community College Avenue
Cleveland, OH 44115
216-987-4200
www.tri-c.cc.oh.us

David Myers College
112 Prospect Avenue
Cleveland, OH 44115-1096
216-696-9000 or 1-877-DNMYERS
www.dnmyers.edu

Franklin University
201 South Grant Avenue
Columbus, OH 43215
614-341-6300 or 1-877-341-6300
www.franklin.edu

Columbus State Community College
550 East Spring Street
Columbus, OH 43215
614-287-5353 or 1-800-621-6407
www.cscc.edu

Ohio State University
Columbus Campus
1800 Cannon Drive
Columbus, OH 43210-1200
614-292-OHIO
www.osu.edu

Sinclair Community College
444 West Third Street
Dayton, OH 45402
937-512-2500
-or-
1-800-315-3000
www.sinclair.edu

Lorain County Community College
1005 Abbe Road North
Elyria, OH 44035-1691
1-800-995-LCCC
www.lorainccc.edu

Terra State Community College
2830 Napolean Road
Fremont, OH 43420-9670
419-334-8400
-or-
866-AT-TERRA
www.terra.cc.oh.us

Miami University-Hamilton Campus
1601 Peck Boulevard
Hamilton, OH 45011
513-785-3000
www.ham.muohio.edu

Cuyahoga Community College, Eastern
Campus
4250 Richmond Road
Highland Hills, OH 44122
216-987-2000
www.tri-c.cc.oh.us

Lakeland Community College
7700 Clocktower Drive
Kirtland, OH 44094-5198
440-953-7000 or 1-800-589-8520
www.lakeland.cc.oh.us

Hocking Technical College
3301 Hocking Parkway
Nelsonville, OH 45764-9704
740-753-3591
www.hocking.edu

Cuyahoga Community College, Western
Campus
11000 Pleasant Valley Road
Parma, OH 44130
216-987-5000
www.tri-c.cc.oh.us

Edison State Community College
1973 Edison Drive
Piqua, OH 45358
937-778-8600
www.edison.cc.oh.us

University of Rio Grande
Rio Grande, OH 45674
740-245-5353
www.urgrgcc.edu

Jefferson Community College
4000 Sunset Boulevard
Steubenville, OH 43952-3598
740-264-5591
-or-
800-68-COLLEGE
www.jeffersoncc.org

University of Toledo
2081 West Bancroft
Toledo, OH 43606-3390
419-530-4242
www.utoledo.edu

Kent State University, Trumbull Campus
4314 Mahoning Avenue, North West
Warren, OH 44483
330-847-0571

OKLAHOMA

Western Oklahoma State College
2801 North Main Street
Altus, OK 73521
580-477-2000
www.western.cc.ok.us

Rogers State College
1701 West Will Rogers Boulevard
Claremore, OH 74017
918-343-7777
www.rsu.edu

University of Central Oklahoma
100 North University Drive
Edmond, OH 73034
405-974-2000
www.ucok.edu

University of Oklahoma
660 Parrington Oval
Norman, OH 73019-4076
405-325-2252
www.ou.edu

Oklahoma City Community College
7777 South May Avenue
Oklahoma City, OH 73159-4444
405-682-1611
www.okc.cc.ok.us

University of Tulsa
600 South College Avenue
Tulsa, OH 74104
800-331-3050 or 918-631-2000
www.tulsa.edu

OREGON

Lane Community College
4000 East 30th Avenue
Eugene, OR 97405
541-747-4501
www.lanecc.edu

Real Estate and Insurance Schools of
    Oregon
1133 South Riverside Avenue, Suite 8
Medford, OR 97501-7807
541-772-1171

Clackamas Community College
19600 South Molalla Avenue
Oregon City, OR 97045
503-657-6958
www.clackamas.cc.or.us

Advanced Educational System
10225 Southwest Parkway
Portland, OR 97225
503-297-1344

Century 21 Peninsula School of Real Estate
8040 North Lombard Street
Portland, OR 97203
503-286-5826

Portland Community College
P.O. 19000
Portland, OR 97280-0990
503-244-6111
www.pcc.edu

Professional Trainers
533 Southeast Main Street
Roseburg, OR 97470
541-672-9200

Century 21 Elite School of Real Estate
58147 South Columbia River Highway
St. Helens, OR 97051
503-397-5023

Center for Professional Studies
1822 Lancaster Drive Northeast
Salem, OR 97305-9730
503-371-4471

Chemeketa Community College
4000 Lancaster Drive NE
Salem, OR 97309-7070
503-399-5006

Norman F. Webb Real Estate Courses
1112 Twelfth Street Southeast
Salem, OR 97302
503-364-0881

PENNSYLVANIA

Northampton Community College
3825 Green Pond Road
Bethlehem, PA 18020
610-861-5300
www.northampton.edu

Montgomery County Community College
340 DeKalb Pike
Blue Bell, PA 19422
215-641-6300
www.mc3.edu

Clarion University of Pennsylvania
Clarion, PA 16214
800-672-7171
www.clarion.edu

Penn State-Erie Behrend College
Station Road
Erie, PA 16563-0195
814-898-6100
www.immaculata.edu

St. Francis College
180 Remsen Street
P.O. Box 600
Loretto, PA 15940
814-472-3000
www.sfcpa.edu

Robert Morris College
881 Narrows Run Road
Moon Township, PA 15108-1189
412-262-8206
www.robert-morris.edu

Luzerne County Community College
Nanticoke, PA 18634-9804
717-740-7336
www.luzerne.edu

Bucks County Community College
Newtown, PA 18940-1525
215-968-8119
www.bucks.edu

Community College of Philadelphia
1700 Spring Garden Street
Philadelphia, PA 19130
215-751-8010
www.ccp.cc.pa.us

Greater Philadelphia Realty Board School
2010 Rhawn Street
Philadelphia, PA 19152
215-722-3400

Temple University
1801 North Broad Street
Philadelphia, PA 19122-6096
215-204-7000
www.temple.edu

University of Pennsylvania
3451 Walnut Street
Philadelphia, PA 19104-6376
215-898-5000
www.upenn.edu

Community College of Allegheny
800 Allegheny Avenue
Pittsburgh, PA 15233
412-325-6614
www.ccac.edu

Duquesne University
600 Forbes Avenue
Pittsburgh, PA 15282
412-396-6000
800-456-0590
www.duq.edu

University of Pittsburgh
Pittsburgh Campus
Bruce Hall, 2nd Floor
Pittsburgh, PA 15260
412-624-7488
www.pitt.edu

Lehigh Carbon Community College
Schnecksville, PA 18078-2598
610-799-1134
www.lccc.edu

Shippensburg University of Pennsylvania
1871 Old Main Drive
Shippensburg, PA 17257
717-477-1111
www.ship.edu

Westmoreland County Community College
Youngwood, PA 15697-1895
724-925-4000
www.westmoreland.cc.pa.us

RHODE ISLAND
Community College of Rhode Island
Knight Campus
Warwick, RI 02886-1807
401-825-1000
www.ccri.cc.ri.us

SOUTH CAROLINA

Real Estate School of South Carolina
10 Diamond Lane, Intersection Center
Columbia, SC 29210-7017
803-731-0654
888-319-0654
www.scinst.com

University of South Carolina
Columbia, SC 29208
803-777-7000
www.sc.edu

Wyatt Institute of Real Estate
710 East North Street
Greenville, SC 29601
864-233-1514
-or-
800-922-9252
www.wyattinstitute.com

Fortune School of Real Estate
P.O. Box 3845
Myrtle Beach, SC 29578
843-236-1131
http://re-school.com

Coastal Carolina University
P.O. Box 261954
Myrtle Beach, SC 29528-6054
843-347-3161
www.coastal.edu

Orangeburg-Calhoun Technical College
3250 Saint Matthews Road
Orangeburg, SC 29118
803-536-0311
800-813-6519
www.octech.org

LaMont School of Real Estate
P.O. Box 152
Huron, SD 57350
800-503-2121

University of South Dakota
414 East Clark Street
Vermillion, SD 57069
605-677-5011
www.usd.edu

Loren Anderson Seminars
122 West Third Street
Yankton, SD 57078
800-657-5892
www.yanktohomes.com

TENNESSEE

North Central Institute
168 Jack Miller Boulevard
Clarksville, TN 37042
931-431-9700
www.nci.edu

Jackson State Community College
2046 North Parkway
Jackson, TN 38301
901-424-3520
www.jscc.cc.tn.us

East Tennessee State University
P.O. Box 70267
Johnson City, TN 37614-0054
423-439-1000
www.etsu.edu

Pellissippi State Technical Community
    College
10915 Hardin Valley Road
Knoxville, TN 37933-0990
865-694-6400
www.pstcc.tn.us

University of Tennessee, Knoxville
320 Student Services Building
Knoxville, TN 37996
865-974-2184
www.utlc.edu

University of Memphis
159 Administration Building
Memphis, TN 38152
901-678-2111
www.memphis.com

Middle Tennessee State University
Murfreesboro, TN 37132
615-898-2111
www.mtsu.edu

Motlow State Community College
26015 Ledford Mill Road
Tullahoma, TN 37388
931-393-1500
www.mscc.cc.tn.us

TEXAS

Amarillo College
P.O. Box 447
Amarillo, TX 79178-0001
806-371-5000
www.actx.edu

University of Texas at Arlington
701 South Nedderman
P.O. Box 19120
Arlington, TX 76019
817-272-2222
www.uta.edu

Trinity Valley Community College
100 Cardinal Drive
Athens, TX 75751-2765
903-675-6357
www.tvcc.cc.tx.us

Austin Community College
5930 Middle Fiskville Road
Austin, TX 78752-4390
512-223-7000
www.austin.cc.tx.us

Lamar University—Beaumont
P.O. Box 10009
Beaumont, TX 77710
409-880-8888
www.theinstitute.lamar.edu

Blinn College
Brenham Campus
902 College Avenue
Brenham, TX 77833
979-821-0338
www.blinncol.edu

Panola College
1109 West Panola
Carthage, TX 75633
903-693-2037
www.panola.cc.tx.us

Texas A&M University
College Station, TX 77843
979-845-1031
www.tamu.edu

Montgomery College
3200 College Park Drive
Conroe, TX 77384
936-273-7000
www.nhmccd.edu

Del Mar College
101 Baldwin Blvd.
Corpus Christi, TX 78404-3897
361-698-1200
800-652-3357
www.delmar.edu

Navarro College
3200 West Seventh Avenue
Corsicana, TX 75110
903-874-6501
800-NAVARRO
www.nav.cc.tx.us

Richland College
12800 Abrams Road
Dallas, TX 75243-2199
972-238-6106
www.rlc.dcccd.edu

Southern Methodist University
6425 Boaz Lane
Dallas, TX 75205
214-768-2058
800-652-3357
www.smu.edu

Grayson County College
Denison, TX 75020
903-465-6030
www.grayson.edu

University of North Texas
P.O. Box 311277
Denton, TX 76203
940-565-2000
www.unt.edu

El Paso Community College
P.O. Box 20500
El Paso, TX 7998
915-831-2000
www.epcc.edu

University of Texas at El Paso
500 West University Avenue
El Paso, TX 79968
915-747-5000
www.utep.edu

Texas Christian University
2800 S. University Drive
Fort Worth, TX 76129
817-257-7000
800-TCU-FROG
www.tcu.edu

North Central Texas College
1525 W. California Street
Gainesville, TX 76240-4699
940-668-7731
www.nctc.cc.tx.us

Hill College of the Hill Junior College District
P.O. Box 619
Hillsboro, TX 76645-0619
254-582-2555
www.hill-college.cc.tx.us

Houston Community College System
P.O. Box 7849
Houston, TX 77270-7849
713-718-2000
www.hccs.cc.tx.us

North Harris Montgomery Community
College District
250 North Sam Houston Parkway East
Houston, TX 77060
281-260-3500
800-96-STARS
www.nhmccd.cc.tx.us

San Jacinto College-North Campus
Houston, TX 77049-4599
281-458-4050
www.sjcd.cc.tx.us

San Jacinto College-South Campus
Houston, TX 77089-6099
281-922-3431
www.sjcd.cc.tx.us

Spencer School of Real Estate
1700 El Camino Real
Houston, TX 77058
713-480-7711

North Lake College
5001 N. MacArthur Blvd
Irving, TX 75038-3899
972-273-3000
http://nlc.dcccd.edu

Schreiner College
2100 Memorial Boulevard
Kerrville, TX 78028
800-896-5411
www.schreiner.edu

Kilgore College
1100 Broadway
Kilgore, TX 75662-3299
903-984-8351
www.kilgore.cc.tx.us

Central Texas College
P.O. Box 1800
Killeen, TX 76540-1800
254-526-7161
1-800-223-4760 (in state)
1-800-729-3348 (out of state)
www.ctcd.cc.tx.us

Laredo Community College
West End Washington Street
Laredo, TX 78040-4395
956-722-0521
www.laredo.cc.tx.us

South Plains College Levelland Campus
1401 South College Ave.
Levelland, TX 79336
806-894-9611
www.spc.cc.tx.us

Angelina College
P.O. Box 1768
Lufkin, TX 75902-1768
963-633-5212
www.angelina.cc.tx.us

Collin County Community College
2200 West University Drive
McKinney, TX 75069
214-495-5780
www.ccccd.edu

Northeast Texas Community College
P.O. Box 1307
Mount Pleasant, TX 75456-1307
903-572-1911
www.ntcc.cc.tx.us

Paris Junior College
2400 Clarksville Street.
Paris, TX 75460
903-785-7661
1-800-232-5804
www.paris.cc.tx.us

San Jacinto College-Central Campus
8060 Spencer Highway
Pasadena, TX 77501-2007
281-476-1819
www.sjcd.cc.tx.us

Angelo State University
2601 West Avenue N
San Angelo, TX 76909
915-942-2185
www.angelo.edu

St. Philips College
1801 Martin Luther King Drive
San Antonio, TX 78203
210-531-4831
www.accd.edu/spc

Texarkana College
2500 North Robison Road
Texarkana, TX 75599-0001
903-838-4541
www.tc.cc.tx.us

College of the Mainland
1200 Amburn Road
Texas City, TX 77591-2499
409-938-1211
www.collegeofthemainland.com

Tyler Junior College
P.O. Box 9020
Tyler, TX 75711-9020
903-510-2399
www.tyler.cc.tx.us

Victoria College
2200 East Red River
Victoria, TX 77901-4494
361-572-6407
www.vc.cc.tx.us

Baylor University
P.O. Box 98004
Waco, TX 76798
800-229-5678
www.baylor.edu

McLennan Community College
1400 College Drive
Waco, TX 76708-1499
817-299-8657

UTAH
Utah Valley State College
800 West University Parkway
Orem, UT 84058-5999
801-222-8000
www.uvsc.edu

Brigham Young University
Provo, UT 84602
801-378-INFO
-or-
1-801-378-4636
www.uvsc.edu

O'Brien Schools
575 East 4500 South
Salt Lake City, UT 84107
801-266-5613

Salt Lake Community College
4600 South Redwood Road
P.O. Box 30808
Salt Lake City, UT 84130-0808
801-957-4297
www.slcc.edu

Stringham Real Estate School, Inc.
5248 South Pinemont Drive, #C250
Salt Lake City, UT 84123
801-269-8889
www.stringham.com

Wardley Real Estate School
2822 South Redwood Road
Salt Lake City, UT 84119
801-533-8378

VIRGINIA
Northern Virginia Community College
8333 Little River Turnpike
Annandale, VA 22003-3796
703-323-3000
www.nv.cc.va.us

Piedmont Virginia Community College
501 College Drive
Charlottesville, VA 22902-8714
804-977-3900
www.pvcc.cc.va.us

John Tyler Community College
13101 Jefferson Davis Highway
Chester, VA 23831-5399
804-796-4000
www.jt.cc.va.us

Eastern Shore Community College
29300 Lankford Highway
Melfa, VA 23410
757-787-5913
www.es.cc.va.us

Alpha College of Real Estate
11861 Canon Boulevard, Suite A
Newport News, VA 23606
757-873-8884
www.anaserve.com/~alphacollege/

Christopher Newport University
1 University Place
Newport News, VA 23606
757-594-7000
www.cnu.edu

Tidewater Community College
7000 College Drive
Portsmouth, VA 23703-6158
757-822-2121
www.tc.cc.va.us

Southwest Virginia Community College
Box 5VCC
Richlands, VA 24641-1510
540-964-2555
www.sw.cc.va.us

J.Sargeant Reynolds Community College
P.O. Box 85622
Richmond, VA 23285-5622
804-371-3029
www.jsr.cc.va.us

Moseley-Flint School of Real Estate
7206 Hull Street Road
Richmond, VA 23235
804-276-7974

Virginia Commonwealth University
821 West Franklin Street, Box 2526
Richmond, VA 23284-9005
804-828-1200
www.vcv.edu

Moseley-Flint School of Real Estate
1727 Peters Creek Road
Roanoke, VA 24017
703-562-2575

Alpha Omega College of Real Estate
2697 International Parkway
Parkway 4, Suite 180
Virginia Beach, VA 23452
757-427-1740

Wytheville Community College
1000 East Main St.
Wytheville, VA 24382-3308
540-223-4755
www.wc.cc.va.us

WASHINGTON

Green River Community College
12401 Southeast 320th Street
Auburn, WA 98092-3699
253-833-9111
www.greenriver.ctc.edu

Bellevue Community College
3000 Landerholm Circle South East
Bellevue, WA 98007
425-564-2222
www.bcc.ctc.edu

Olympic College
1600 Chester Avenue
Bremerton, WA 98337-1699
360-475-7200
www.oc.ctc.edu

Lower Columbia College
1600 Maple
P.O. Box 3010
Longview, WA 98632
360-577-2311
http://lcc.ctc.edu

Columbia Basin College
2600 North 20th Avenue
Pasco, WA 99301
509-547-0511
www.cbc2.org

Renton Technical College
3000 Northeast Fourth Street
Renton, WA 98056-4195
425-235-2352
www.renton-tc.ctc.edu

Century 21 Real Estate Academy
1800 International Boulevard, Suite 1021
Seattle, WA 98188
206-248-2100

North Seattle Community College
9600 College Way North
Seattle, WA 98103-3599
206-527-3639
www.gonorth.org

Shoreline Community College
16101 Greenwood Avenue North
Seattle, WA 98133
206-546-4621
www.shoreline.ctc.edu

Spokane Falls Community College
3410 West Fort George Wright Drive
Spokane, WA 99224-5288
509-533-3520
www.sfcc.spokane.cc.wa.us

Pierce College a Fort Steilacoom
9401 Farwest Drive Southwest
Lakewood, WA 98498
253-964-6500
www.pierce.ctc.edu

Yakima Valley Community College
P.O. Box 22520
Yakima, WA 98907-2520
509-574-4600
www.yvcc.cc.wa.us

WEST VIRGINIA

Davis and Elkins College
100 Campus Drive
Elkins, WV 26241-3996
800-624-3157
www.dne.edu

Fairmont State College
1201 Locust Avenue
Fairmont, WV 26554-2496
304-367-4141
-or-
800-641-5678
www.fscwv.edu

Marshall University
400 Hal Greer Boulevard
Huntington, WV 25755-2020
304-696-3160
www.marshall.edu

WISCONSIN
Chippewa Valley Technical College
620 West Clairemont Avenue
Eau Claire, WI 54701-6120
715-833-6246
www.chippewa.tec.wi.us

Madison Area Technical College
3550 Anderson Street
Madison, WI 53704
608-246-6100
-or-
800-322-6282
www.madison.tech.wi.us

University of Wisconsin - Madison
750 University Avenue
Madison, WI 53706
608-262-3961
www.wiscinfo.doit.wisc.edu/bschool

Milwaukee Area Technical College
700 West State Street
Milwaukee, WI 53233-1443
414-297-6301
www.matc.edu

Robbins & Lloyd School of Real Estate and
Insurance
5309 North 118th Court
Milwaukee, WI 53225
414-464-0800
www.robbinslloyd.com

University of Wisconsin - Milwaukee
P.O. Box 413
Milwaukee, WI 53201
414-229-3800
www.uwm.edu

Nicolet Area Technical College
Rhinelander, WI 54501-0518
715-365-4451
www.nicoletcollege.com

Waukesha County Technical College
800 Main St.
Pewaukee, WI 53072
262-691-5566
www.waukesha.tec.wi.us

Wauwatosa Real Estate Institute, Inc.
11622 West North Avenue
Wauwatoga, WI 53226
414-476-797

WYOMING
Academy Real Estate School
P.O. Box 6444
Rock Springs, WY 82901
307-382-4841

Appendix D

Sample Contract

FOLLOWING IS a listing contract used by agents in Nebraska. It is provided here to give you a sense of the type of legal paperwork that is an essential part of every real estate professional's job.

THIS IS A LEGALLY BINDING AGREEMENT,
IF NOT UNDERSTOOD, SEEK LEGAL ADVICE.

This contract form has been prepared by the Nebraska Real Estate Commission. It is intended to include provisions common to most transactions. Its use is not mandatory and it will not be suitable for contracts having or requiring unusual provisions.

Commission rates and contract terms are not regulated by law and are subject to negotiation between the Real Estate Broker and the Seller.

EXCLUSIVE RIGHT-TO-SELL LISTING CONTRACT

(Seller) [Name(s) of Owner(s)]_____

contracts with_____

(Broker) [Broker's Name or Firm and Address]_____

_____

_____

_____

_____

for the purposes and under the terms set forth below with my specific Seller's Limited Agent to be_____ and such other affiliated licensees of Broker as may be assigned by Broker in writing, if needed as exclusive Seller's Limited Agents. The affiliated licensee(s) named in this paragraph and the Seller's Limited Agents who may be appointed by the Broker are collectively referred to in this Listing Contract as Seller's Limited Agents. All responsibilities and duties of Broker shall also be the responsibilities and duties of the Seller's Limited Agent:

1. Purpose of Agency. The purpose of this sole and exclusive right-to-sell agency contract ("Listing Contract") is to engage the efforts of Broker to accomplish the sale of the Real Property legally described as:

   also known as_____
   (Street Address)

   _____
   (City)   (State)

   together with any items of Personal Property to be conveyed pursuant to Paragraph 5 (collectively referred to as the "Property").

2. Effect of this Listing Contract. By contracting with Broker, Seller agrees to conduct all negotiations for the Sale of the Property through Seller's Limited Agent and to refer to Seller's Limited Agent all inquiries received in any form from any source during the term of this Contract.

3. The Listing Period. This Contract shall begin _____, _____, and shall continue through _____, _____. (This is referred to as the "Listing Period.")

4. Price and Terms. The Offering Price for the Property shall be $_____ on the following Terms:

5. Price to Include. The Price shall include all attached fixtures, except _____. The following Personal Property is also included:

6. Title. Seller represents to Broker that title to the Property is solely in Seller's name. Seller shall deliver to Broker, upon request, copies of all relevant title materials. Seller represents that there are no known encroachments affecting this Property, except (If none, state "None"):

   Seller agrees to convey marketable title by warranty deed or_____.
   If the Property has been or will be assessed for local improvements installed, under construction, or ordered by public authority at the time of signing a Purchase Agreement, Seller will be responsible for payment of same.

Broker may terminate this Listing Contract upon written notice to Seller that title is not satisfactory to Broker.

7. Evidence of Title. Seller agrees to convey a marketable title to Buyer, evidenced by a policy of title insurance or an abstract certified to date.

8. Possession. Possession of the Property shall be delivered to Buyer on _____, _____.

9. Material Defects and Indemnification. Seller represents to the Broker solely for the purposes of this Listing Contract that he or she has completed or will promptly complete the Seller Property Condition Disclosure Statement fully and correctly to the best of the Seller's knowledge. Seller further states that all oral representations made to Seller's Limited Agent are accurate. Seller's Limited Agent shall not receive any offers to purchase until the Seller Property Condition Disclosure Statement is complete.

Seller agrees to indemnify and hold harmless Broker (Listing Company) and any subagents, from any claim that may be made against the Listing Company or subagents by reason of the Seller having breached the terms of this paragraph. In addition, Seller agrees to pay attorney fees and associated costs reasonably incurred by Broker to enforce this indemnity. Seller agrees that any defects of a material nature (including, but not limited to, structural defects; soil conditions; violations of health, zoning or building laws; and nonconforming uses or zoning variances) actually known by Seller's Limited Agent must be disclosed by Seller's Limited Agent to any prospective Buyer.

10. Compensation of Broker. In consideration of services to be performed by Seller's Limited Agent, Seller agrees to pay Broker a commission of _____, payable upon the happening of any of the following:

   (a) If during the term of the listing, Seller, Broker or any other person:

      (1) sells the Property; or

      (2) finds a Buyer who is ready, willing and able to purchase the Property at the above price and terms or for any other price and terms to which Seller agrees to accept; or

      (3) finds a Buyer who is granted an option to purchase or enters into a lease with option to purchase and the option is subsequently exercised; or

   (b) If this agreement is revoked or violated by Seller; or

   (c) If Broker is prevented in closing the Sale of this Property by existing claims, liens, judgments, or suits pending against this Property, or Seller thereof; or

   (d) If Broker is unfairly hindered by Seller in the showing of or attempting to sell this Property.

Or,

    (e) If within _____ days after the expiration of this Listing Contract, Seller sells this Property to any person found during the term of this listing, or due to Broker's efforts or advertising, under this Listing Contract, unless this Property is listed with another Broker.

11. **Limitation on Broker's Compensation.** Broker may accept compensation when Broker or affiliated licensee (other than Seller's Limited Agent), is serving as a Buyer's Agent. In all other cases, Broker shall not accept compensation from the Buyer, the Buyer's agent, or any entity participating in or providing services for the Sale without written agreement of Seller.

12. **Cooperating with Other Brokers.** Broker may accept the assistance and cooperation of other brokers who will be acting as subagents of the seller or as agents for a Buyer. If Broker participates in a local multiple listing service Broker shall submit the Property to such listing service. Seller authorizes Broker to compensate from the amount described in paragraph 10: ( ) seller's subagent; ( ) buyer's agent; ( ) agents acting for both the buyer and the seller-dual agents.

13. **Forfeiture of Earnest Money.** In the event of forfeiture of the earnest money made by a prospective Buyer, the monies received, after expenses incurred by Broker, shall be divided between Broker and Seller, one-half thereof to Broker, but not to exceed the commission agreed upon herein, and the balance to Seller.

14. **Cost of Services.** Broker shall bear all expenses incurred by Broker, if any, to market the Property and to compensate cooperating brokers, if any. Broker will not obtain or order any products or services to be paid by Seller unless Seller agrees. Broker shall not be obligated to advance funds for the benefit of Seller.

15. **Maintenance of the Property.** Seller agrees to maintain until delivery of possession, the heating, air conditioning, water heater, sewer, plumbing and electrical systems and any built-in appliances in good and reasonable working condition. Seller further agrees to hold Broker harmless from any and all causes of action, loss, damage, or expense Broker may be subjected to arising in connection with this section. Seller also agrees that Broker shall not be responsible for maintenance of the Property.

16. **Nondiscrimination.** The undersigned Seller and Broker acknowledge, by their respective signature hereon, that the law prohibits discrimination for or against any person because of race, color, religion, sex, handicap, familial status, or national origin.

17. **Escrow Closing.** Seller agrees that the closing of any sale made by Broker may be handled by an Escrow Agent and authorizes Broker to transfer all earnest monies, down

payments and other trust funds to the Escrow Agent along with documents and other items received by Broker related to the sale. The cost of the Escrow Closing shall be paid by Seller or as negotiated with the Buyer in the Purchase Agreement.

18. Smoke Detectors. Seller agrees to install at Seller's expense any smoke detectors required by law.

19. "For Sale" Sign Permitted. Seller gives permission to Broker to place a "For Sale" and a "Sold" sign on the Property and to use a "Lock Box."

20. Duties and Responsibilities of Seller's Limited Agent. Seller's Limited Agent shall have the following duties and obligations:

    (a) To perform the terms of this agreement;

    (b) To exercise reasonable skill and care for Seller;

    (c) To promote the interest of Seller with the utmost good faith, loyalty and fidelity including:

        (1) Seeking the price and terms which are acceptable to Seller except that Seller's Limited Agent shall not be obligated to seek additional offers to purchase the property while the property is subject to a contract for sale;

        (2) Presenting all written offers to and from Seller in a timely manner regardless of whether the property is subject to a contract for sale;

        (3) Disclosing in writing to Seller all adverse material facts actually known by Seller's Limited Agent; and

        (4) Advising Seller to obtain expert advice as to material matters of that which Seller's Limited Agent knows but the specifics of which are beyond the expertise of Seller's Limited Agent;

    (d) To account in a timely manner for all money and property received;

    (e) To comply with the requirements of agency relationships as defined in Neb. Rev. Stat. 76-2401 through 76-2430, the Nebraska Real Estate License Act, and any rules or regulations promulgated pursuant to such sections or act; and

    (f) To comply with any applicable federal, state, and local laws, rules, regulations, and ordinances, including fair housing and civil rights statutes and regulations.

21. Confidential Information. Seller's Limited Agent shall not disclose any confidential information about Seller, without Seller's written permission, unless disclosure is required by statute, rule, or regulation, or failure to disclose the information would constitute fraudulent misrepresentation. Seller's Limited Agent is required to disclose adverse material facts to any prospective buyer. Adverse material facts may include any environmental hazards affecting the property which are required by law to be disclosed, physical condition of the

property, any material defects in the property, any material defects in the title to the property, or any material limitation on Seller's ability to perform under the terms of the contract.

22. Modification of this Listing Contract. No modification of this Listing Contract shall be valid, unless made in writing and signed by the parties.

23. Release of Information. Seller authorizes Broker to obtain any information relating to utility expenses and all pertinent information regarding the present mortgage(s) or Deed(s) of Trust on this Property including existing balance, interest rate, monthly payment, balance in escrow account and pay off amount. Seller authorizes the dissemination of sales information including selling price and terms after closing of the transaction.

24. Entire Agreement. This Listing Contract constitutes the entire Contract between the parties and any prior negotiations or agreements, whether oral or written, are not valid unless set forth in this Contract.

25. Copies of Agreement. This Listing Contract is executed in multiple copies and Seller acknowledges receipt of a copy signed by the Broker or Broker's affiliated licensee.

Signed this_____ day of _____ ,_____.

_____
(Name of Broker or Firm)

_____
(Address)   (Phone No.)

By _____
   (Affiliated Licensee's Signature)   (Date)

_____
(Name of Seller(s)—Type or Print)

_____
(Seller(s) Signature/SS#/Fed ID#)   (Date)

_____
(Seller(s) Signature/SS#/Fed ID#)   (Date)

_____
(Seller(s) Address)

_____
            (City)   (State)   (Zip)

_____
(Residence)   (Business)   (Seller Phone)

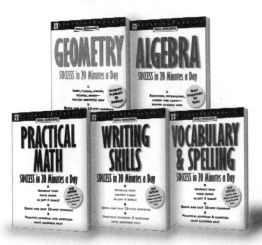

Achieve Test Success
With LearningExpress

Our acclaimed series of academic and other job related exam guides are the most sought after resources of their kind. Get the edge with the only exam guides to offer the features that test-takers have come to expect from LearningExpress—The Exclusive LearningExpress Advantage:

Easy to Use & Understand

- **THREE** Complete practice tests based on official exams
- Vital review of skills tested and hundreds of sample questions with full answers and explanations
- The exclusive LearningExpress Test Preparation System—must know exam information, test-taking strategies, customized study planners, tips on physical and mental preparation and more.

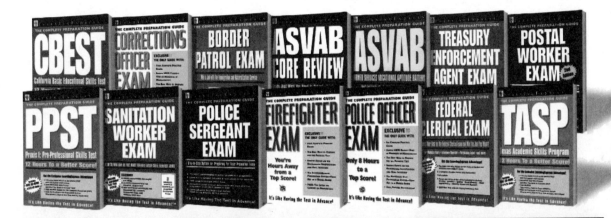

Also available at your local bookstore. Prices Subject to Change Without Notice.